Y0-BNP-613

# 75 STORIES
# AND ILLUSTRATIONS
# FROM EVERYDAY LIFE

by

Erwin L. McDonald

BAKER BOOK HOUSE
Grand Rapids, Michigan

Library of Congress Catalog Card Number: 64-16943

Copyright, 1964, by
Baker Book House Company

*First printing, March 1964*
*Second printing, May 1968*

PHOTOLITHOPRINTED BY CUSHING - MALLOY, INC.
ANN ARBOR, MICHIGAN, UNITED STATES OF AMERICA
1968

TO FIVE WOMEN in my life:

my wife, Mary, who likes to be called Maria; our daughters, Jeannine and Judy; my mother, Rebecca Geneva; and my mother-in-law, Maudie.

# INTRODUCTION

I have known the author from boyhood — *his* boyhood. He wasn't around in *my* boyhood, which was spent in the county of his birth, Pope County, Arkansas. I am proud of this lad from London (one of Pope's smallest villages). He has the rare gift of seeing sermons in stones. From simple incidents in the life of the countryside and later the throbbing life of the State Capital, he has drawn impressive lessons. I didn't want to lay his manuscript down till I had read all of his seventy-five stories. He and I knew a Baptist preacher in our youth, who could say incisive things ungrammatically. (I sometimes suspected his bad English was intentional.) One of his capsules: "A man don't know nothing he didn't learn." It is one text my fellow Londoner did not use, but the truth expressed by our preacher friend is found in the wisdom these episodes reveal.

These stories also reflect the unique gift that the Baptist journalist Erwin McDonald himself enjoys. He has imparted to the readers in this remarkable collection the impressions of a sensitive Christian, gained from the simple experiences of daily life.

This is a bonanza of sermon material for the preacher and a fine source of conversational content for the layman. I recommend it unreservedly for the person who wants to embellish his own conversations, add charm to any public addresses he is called upon to make. However, stories springing from contemporaneous happenings are embossed with a knowledge of the Bible and he adopts appropriate passages to fortify the moral and religious principles which are obviously directing and strengthening his own life.

—Brooks Hays

# CONTENTS

# 75 STORIES AND ILLUSTRATIONS
## FROM EVERYDAY LIFE

## 1. Another's Push

As I came out of a Little Rock bank one day recently, I noticed an elderly man just a step or two behind me. The first of two doors leading to the street was a "push" door and I held it till the man could take it. The next was a "pull" door. I opened the door and stood back for the man to pass.

But he would not accept my courtesy. "Go ahead, Sir," he replied, and then he added: "I never like to go through on another fellow's push!"

We were strangers, but I must confess that I was a little taken aback by his reaction to my intended goodwill.

As I thought of the experience, I recalled something I had seen months ago while attending a special service in a distant city. Several men were on the program and sat together on the platform. One of them, the victim of a stroke some months before, was largely disabled and seemed to have some difficulty as he started to leave the platform at the close of the service. One of his friends who had shared the platform honors, an able-bodied, young man, instinctively took the disabled man by the arm to help him.

But the stricken man recoiled, jerking his arm away from the would-be helper, and storming so that many of us in the auditorium heard it: "Leave me alone!"

Still later, as I passed the offended man in the vestibule, he was talking about the "incident" to one who had formerly been associated with him and I heard him say: "That made me so mad!"

One does not have to be a psychologist to understand how this could happen. The man had lived a lifetime of being independent and he still had his pride and his spirit of independence, even though his body was physically broken.

The man who would not walk through the door I had opened for him may have been more self-conscious of his grey hair than he realized, and he may have had the mistaken idea that a younger man was trying to help him because the younger man thought he was getting too old and decrepit to help himself.

Self-reliance is a wonderful thing, if it is not carried too far. And a certain amount of pride is all right. But there is a self-reliance that damns and there is a pride that goeth before a fall.

Any who are so self-reliant that they make the mistake of regarding themselves as self-sufficient, shut themselves off from God and the help that all of us need, every breath we take.

## 2. Praying It Through

The young theolog had a bad case of the blues. He lacked the radiance he felt he should possess as a Christian. Finally he decided he would lock himself in his room and "pray it through."

But that did not take long. At the end of ten minutes he was terribly conscious of the hardness of the floor against his knees, and the fact that he had just about prayed everything he knew to pray. Also he was conscious that he didn't feel any better.

It was a Saturday afternoon and the Seminary campus where he was a student was almost deserted. In his loneliness he decided to seek somebody else who was lonely. So he went to General Hospital at the regular visiting hour.

There he found several patients in a men's ward who had no company among the large number of hospital visitors. They were glad indeed to have his visit. Before he left he had won three lost men to Christ.

Needless to say, he left the hospital in a far different

mood from the mood that possessed him when he had entered. Now he had the radiance he had sought to no avail in his prayers.

Today the young theologian is many years older and has long been an outstanding preacher and soul-winner, for he is Dr. Ralph Herring, formerly pastor of First Baptist Church, Winston-Salem, North Carolina. But he has never forgotten the lesson he learned that lonely Saturday afternoon in Louisville, Kentucky, according to his personal testimony given recently.

There is often a great need for us to give feet to the prayers we pray. Sometimes the thing we need most of all is to get up out of our chairs, or maybe, even off our knees, and do something.

A man trapped on an ice floe dropped to his knees to pray for God's deliverance. But a realistic brother on shore who saw that there was still not too much distance between the floating ice and the shore for his friend to jump to safety called to him to get off his knees and jump while there was still time.

Any time of the year is a good time to match our praying with Christian deeds. But no time is better than now. The great tragedy is that we so often put off to another day carrying out the good impulses of today. We should be eager to be used of God in the answering of our own prayers.

## 3. An Oak or a Squash

"Since my son is unusually bright," said the father to the college president as he had come to enroll the young man in college, "I wonder if you could not let him finish his courses in less than the usual time."

"It all depends on what you want to make of your son," the wise president countered. "If you want him to be an oak, it will take much time. But if you will be satisfied for him to be a squash, we can have him ready in short order."

Sometimes a young person just out of high school will say: "Why waste four years of my life going to college when I can take a short course and get a job?"

The answer to this question is obvious. If all one wants is the technical training that will make one proficient with certain machines, and if one is not concerned about having a broad, general education that will equip one with its expansion of vision and understanding and bolster one's ability to make wise decisions, college is a waste of time.

This is not to say that only those who go to college can be educated. Many who for one reason or another never qualify for college degrees are self-educated. And far too many go through college and receive degrees without getting an education. But, whether one gets his learning primarily in schools and colleges or acquires it on his own, the point is that it cannot be had quickly or easily.

Acquiring an education is far more than spending four or more years in college or university. It is a life-long pursuit. And, of course, it takes in far more than books, including all the personal experiences one has along the way.

Not the least important factor in true education is religion. Jesus, the Master Teacher and the source of light and love, sets down the basic principle for those who would be wise:

*Then spake Jesus again unto them, saying, I am the light of the world: he that followeth me shall not walk in darkness, but shall have the light of life. . . .*

*Then said Jesus to those Jews which believed on him, If ye continue in my word, then are ye my disciples indeed;*

*And ye shall know the truth, and the truth shall make you free (8:12, 31-32).*

Just as many people are unhealthy physically because they ignore or break the laws of health, many are warped in their lives because they try to take spiritual and mental short cuts. There is no substitute for learning daily in the school of Christ and the development of our characters takes time.

## 4. She Needed to Give

On what used to be called Armistice Day (now Veterans' Day) the papers carried the sad story of a father in Newark, New Jersey, stabbing his twelve-year-old daughter to death in an argument over donating food for a school Thanksgiving basket for the poor.

The children at school had each been asked to bring something, and Mildred Campbell, a sixth grader, asked her father, forty-seven-year-old Robert Campbell, for a box of gelatin or a bag of walnuts.

As the disabled head of a family on relief — a family including six children — the father refused. "We need it more than they do," he said.

In the argument that ensued, the father is reported to have plunged a paring knife into the chest of the little girl, killing her instantly.

The fact that the father was an epileptic and unemployable adds to the pathos.

Despite the fact she was from a relief family, Mildred had felt the necessity of giving something. It may be she could not stand the embarrassment of being one, perhaps the only one in her class, who would give nothing.

Or she may have had the higher motive of a Christian, desiring out of her love and concern for those even no less fortunate than herself and her family, to share what she had. In that case she must have been a kindred spirit with those Christians of another age of whom it was said: ". . . in a great trial of affliction the abundance of their joy and their deep poverty abounded unto the riches of their liberality. For to their power . . . and beyond their power they were willing of themselves; praying us with much intreaty that we would receive the gift, and take upon us the fellowship of the ministering to the saints."

The one who withholds all for self will surely become stagnant if not bitter. But the one who, out of love, even

though the personal need be great, gives, is not likely
ever to be either stagnant or bitter or miserable.

Yes, Mildred needed to give. She needed to give more
than she needed a new dress or new shoes or better balanced
meals. For Mildred was a human being.

## 5. "No Escape from Life"

The pressure and grind of meeting deadlines to get out
even a small daily newspaper can get to be mighty routine
and monotonous. I learned this first-hand several years ago
while serving as city editor of the Russellville, Arkansas,
*Daily Courier-Democrat.*

We used to conclude our *Courier-Democrat* coffee breaks
with such cracks as: "Well, it's back to the old squirrel
cage!" or "Back to the salt mines!"

There is pressure and grind in daily living. The house
maid who said "Life is *so daily!*" expressed the sentiment
of many.

The ups and downs of life break some people and make
others. If we look upon the serenity and dignity of the
truly great souls, we might be inclined to think that these
have never had any bad breaks. But great character does
not come without hardship.

John Sutherland Bonnell warns in his book, *No Escape
from Life*:

"With every year that passes the necessity for effort on
our part is lessened. Multitudes are living today by the
creed of comfort. We are producing a soft generation. Year
by year new inventions make labor less and less necessary.

"In some of his more recent lectures T. S. Eliot has
warned that even in our pleasures we are eliminating all
necessity for endurance or fatigue. The philosophy of life
of many Americans is to achieve relief from every form of
hardship. Little by little we are beginning to regard struggle,
effort, and self-sacrifice as things to be avoided. We long

for even a greater comfort. But our comforts do not make us happy. Distinguished visitors from India and other Eastern lands have marveled at the mental stress in American life — the surplus of tension and the evidence of mental and physical weariness."

If Paul had been like a lot of us Americans today, he never would have learned to "endure hardship as a good soldier of Jesus Christ." When he prayed three times for the Lord to remove his "thorn in the flesh" and the thorn remained, he would have become a helpless and hopeless invalid.

Those who stop trying because the going gets rough need to lift their eyes from the rough spots in the road to the One whose "grace is sufficient."

. . . *they that wait upon the Lord shall renew their strength . . . (Isa. 40:31).*

## 6. "Try the Spirits"

One of London's (Pope County) frequent attractions on Saturday afternoons back in World War I days was the old-time medicine show featuring "Doc" with his frocktail coat, black bow tie, and persuasive tongue.

"Doc" would park his wagon or truck in the most conspicuous available spot and soon would be surrounded by a great crowd of suckers — pardon me, customers. There were lots of folks to draw, for people from miles around would come in to have "rounds" of corn ground at George Martin's grist mill; or, perhaps, to have mules shod or a plow sharpened at Si Ruble's blacksmith shop; and to stand around and visit together while sipping delicious, self-made fountain cokes at Shrigg Eggleston's, where every one shaved his own ice with a sweat-producing, manual ice shaver.

It didn't take ole "Doc" and his ever-present, blacked-face handyman ("Sold out, Doc!") long to get their "free" vaudeville going. Every little while "Doc" would interrupt the show to make available at a dollar a bottle whatever he had had the most left of from previous sales. One time it might be healing oil "good for man or beast." Or it might be a "tonic" recommended for every condition from jaded appetites to advanced tuberculosis.

One of the really great marvels, it seemed to me at the time, was Dr. Somebody's "Corn Remedy." You didn't even have to pull off your shoe — just drop a few drops on your shoe over a throbbing corn and you would feel immediate relief.

The medicine man has graduated into big-time advertising. Today we are exposed to him constantly on radio and TV and in newspapers and magazines. He still tries to make us feel he has a miraculous product, whether it is tooth paste, shampoo, shaving cream, lipstick or something else he is paid to hawk.

But today the medicine man is not always selling products. Frequently he has turned "statesman" or "preacher" and is telling us what is right and what is wrong and how we are to live and vote and use our influence.

Many are asking, "Who or what can we believe when there are so many claims — so many charges and counter-charges?"

The words of I John 4:1 seem peculiarly appropriate:
*Beloved, believe not every spirit, but try the spirits whether they are of God: because many false prophets are gone out into the world.*


## 7. Mountain Moving

A long time ago, Jesus declared that mountains can be moved by faith — just a little faith — faith as a grain of mustard seed. But that was before the day of bulldozers and caterpillars. Now we have innumerable handy gadgets. We have learned so much about moving mountains that we are rather smug and self-reliant in this technological age.

But take another look at the modern mountain movers. All of their big equipment notwithstanding, faith is still necessary in their business.

Whether it was recognized as such, there was a lot of faith exercised by the men who devised and constructed the modern machinery used by road builders and earth movers. Before they could walk by sight they had to walk by faith. Although they had never seen it, they believed that the equipment which has long since become commonplace among us could be brought into being. Using the materials of the earth, also His creation, they brought the earth-moving equipment to pass.

The inventors of the highway equipment and the highway engineers alike had to have faith in certain basic laws of the physical universe, laws which are also of God's making. They have never been able to revoke or change these laws. Wise men do not try, for to do so is to break themselves.

Modern equipment and the findings of engineering do not constitute an overpass over or around faith. Faith is still essential in moving physical mountains. But it is even more essential in moving spiritual mountains. As Jesus says to this day, a little faith can accomplish miracles. And faith, though it be small in the beginning, can grow to great proportions.

## 8. " . . . Only the Strong . . . "

During the Great Depression of the 1930's one of our young friends who had no job accepted our suggestion and signed up with a large publishing firm to sell books during a summer. The first half day he worked, in our county-seat town of Russellville, he made commissions totalling $25.

Now that was mighty good wages, especially for one who had no income whatever. That was even better than I was earning as city editor of the *Daily Courier-Democrat*. The young fellow was walking on air as he reported to me at noon. I rejoiced with him.

Seeing him a day or two later, I asked him how his work was going, expecting to hear reports of new achievements.

"Oh, I quit!" he reported.

"Quit?" I asked, dumbfounded. "Why in the world would you quit after such a good start?"

It developed that he had run into a shrew of a housewife on his first call out, after his glorious first half a day, and she had bawled him out for knocking on her door and had paid her disrespects to book agents in general and to him in particular.

That was all it had taken to remove this ambitious young man from the book-selling business. He did not have anything else to do, but he quit! His shell was too soft. He just couldn't get up the courage to make another call.

Across the years I have often thought of this young man whose nerve failed him and I have tried to imagine what the story might have been like if he had been able to just "consider the source" in the matter of his "bawling out."

Certainly, this is a cruel, hard world for people with soft shells! And this is no less true for church people than for others. For this reason pastors have a difficult task as they try to lead their members to take seriously their assignment from God himself to be "salesmen for Christ," selling a way of abundant living through Christ.

Christians, of all people, cannot afford to be soft-shelled. We are called to be cross bearers. We are warned by our Lord who sends us out that the going will often be hard. But he has promised us the blessing of his presence and grace that is sufficient.

"The coward never starts, the weak fall by the way, only the strong come through!"

## 9. Blessed Book

*This book contains the mind of God, the state of man, the way of salvation, the doom of sinners, and the happiness of believers. Its doctrines are holy, its precepts are binding, its histories are true, and its decisions are immutable. Read it to be wise, believe it to be safe, and practice it to be holy.*

It has been several years since I first came across this. Who is its author I do not know. But for a long time it has been on a flyleaf of one of my favorite personal possessions — the Scofield Reference Bible which First Baptist Church, Russellville, presented to me upon the occasion of my ordination to the ministry, on May 18, 1938.

Scattered here and there through this Bible out of which I have preached across many years and in several states are many more notes — sermon outlines and personal commentaries — written in the margins.

One Sunday I left this Bible with the desk clerk — a woman — at a hotel while I had lunch in the hotel dining room. Upon returning to pick it up, I was surprised to find the woman diligently turning through it to see what all I had written in it.

I thus witnessed to a person who, as far as I know, I have not yet had the privilege of having in any congregation to which I have preached. It has occurred to me, as it has to you, that it would have been far more profitable for the dear lady to have spent her time centering on what God had written in that blessed book.

In keeping with the statement with which we started this column is this from God himself: "For the word of God is quick, and powerful, and sharper than any two-edged sword, piercing even to the dividing asunder of soul and spirit, and of the joints and marrow, and is a discerner of the thoughts and intents of the heart" (Heb. 4:12).

## 10. Motto on the Wall

Sometimes people you have met or have been associated with remember things about you, your home, or your place of work that you do not expect them to remember. It is surprising, sometimes embarrassing, and, not infrequently, downright deflating to hear someone who knew you " 'way back when . . ." recount something you said or did on an occasion you have long since forgotten — or tried to forget!

On one of my preaching engagements out in the state, a preacher who had met me in my office several months previously was complimenting me for "the motto you have on your wall." He said that he had jotted it down and had used it rather effectively in a sermon.

Now any well-meaning editor would be pleased to know that something he has on his wall, if not something he has put in his paper, has been helpful to somebody. To know that somebody has poked his head in at an editor's door and gone away remembering something besides the usual clutter to be seen there is always heartening. So the brother's comment was greatly appreciated. But for the life of me and all of my forefathers, I could not remember having a motto of any kind on my office wall!

Not wanting to appear any dumber than was absolutely necessary, I did not allow myself to be drawn into a conversation with the preacher friend about the motto. But you may be sure that that was one time this editor was not only willing but glad to head back to his office.

On opening the door, there was the motto, as big as life. It was the Rotary "Four Way Test":

"First, Is it the truth?

"Second, Is it fair to all concerned?

"Third, Will it build good will and better friendships?

"Fourth, Will it be beneficial to all concerned?"

Why had I not remembered? It was not that I was oblivious to the fact that the "Four Way Test" is on my wall. I just had not been thinking of it as constituting a motto.

You do not have to be a Rotarian to practice this wise way of life, which is most consistent with the teachings of Christ. The next time you hear somebody or some organization or some society or race being maligned, you might profitably apply this test in determining whether or not to pass on to somebody else the things you have heard.

## 11. Burned-out Bearings

On a hot summer day in a southern city a giant transport truck came to a screeching stop at the curb and the driver sprang from his cab in anxiety. A rear wheel on his trailer was almost spitting fire.

As soon as the wheel had cooled sufficiently, the driver began the ordeal of taking it off. Before he realized it, quite a crowd had gathered to see what was taking place.

A well known pastor of the city was among the onlookers. According to G. A. Leichliter, executive secretary of the Florida Baptist Foundation, here is what happened:

The preacher began by asking the usual foolish question that is always raised by somebody under such circumstances:

"Has your truck broken down?"

The answer was obvious, but the truck driver was courteous and so he simply replied, "Yes."

Foolish question number two: "What happened to it?"

Courteous reply number two: "A wheel-bearing has burned out."

Then the questioner had still another query of the same class and category:

"What do you suppose would cause that?"

The simple, eloquent answer: "No grease."

The preacher stood in silence for a while, watching the toiling driver who had anything but a cool place to work, up against that simmering wheel. Then the preacher chanced to look at the lettering across the side of the transport. It read: "Standard Oil Company — Lubricants Department."

As he turned away, the preacher soliloquized: "He burned out a bearing hauling grease!"

There are a lot of people today besides truck drivers who are "burning out bearings hauling grease."

Parents who make every sacrifice to provide for their children the things that money can buy but take no thought of their sacred obligation to bring their children up in the fear and admonition of the Lord, certainly come in this category.

"He burned out a bearing hauling grease!"


## 12. "Blur of Motion"

Aeronautic engineers are predicting now that it will soon be possible to fly around the world in commercial transports in fifty-four hours. Wonder how much a trip like that would be worth? Think how interesting it would be to have somebody just back from such a trip tell about all the interesting people and lands he flew over!

Well, of course, this will be or should be a wonderful thing for all of us, if world travelers can learn how to use such rapid transit.

No generation of Americans has ever had so much time of its own as ours. In just a few decades we have moved from a 12-to-14-hour work day to an 8-hour day with two coffee breaks and from a six-day work week to a five-day week. And now there is a lot of talk about a four-day week! But we still have seven days to the week (and weak).

As Claire Cox pointed out the other day in a UPI feature, so far Americans have not been able to settle down and use their new hours and days to much real purpose or satisfaction.

Cox quotes Pastor J. Edward Carothers of the First Methodist Church, Schenectady, New York, as marvelling at how strange it is that with our increase of wealth and devices "we have lost leisure."

"The same technology we use to provide us with a shorter work week we also use to speed us through the air, propel us over the water or down a slope.

"The contemporary picture of the American citizen is a blur of motion."

Man being incurably religious, we can never hope to find true happiness and peace unless our daily and weekly schedules make places for worship of God. People who make of the Lord's day just a day of recreation really should spell the word with a "w" — "wreckreation."

Next to public and private worship we would place, as a most worthy use of our new leisure time, a wholesome interest in people and the world about us. The wife of the busy physician we read about the other day who, with her husband, gets away every few days to spend more time so far back in the woods they cannot have access to telephone or television, or many other modern-day gadgets, but who communes with God's great outdoors, is making good use of leisure time, we'd say.

## 13. Greatest Sayings

According to Theodore Henry Palmquist, pastor of Foundry Church, Washington, D. C., the following are "The Ten Greatest Sayings of Men":

"All things whatsoever ye would that men should do to you, do ye even so to them: for this is the law and the prophets." — Jesus

"Know thyself." — Socrates

"Hatred ceases not by hatred. Hatred ceases by love." — Confucius

"What doth the Lord require of thee but to do justly, and to love mercy and to walk humbly with thy God?" — Micah

"He that findeth his life shall lose it; but he that loseth

his life for my sake shall find it." — Jesus

"There are many members, but one body; therefore, there should be no division in the body, but members should have the same care one for another. And whether one member suffer, all the members suffer with it — or one member prosper all the members rejoice with it. For the body is not one member but many." — Paul

"Act according to laws which can at the same time be made a universal law of conduct." — Emmanuel Kant

"My country is the world and my religion is to do good." — Thomas Paine

"I do not know the method of drawing up an indictment against a whole people." — Edmund Burke

"With malice toward none, with charity for all, with firmness in the right as God gives us to see the right, let us strive on to finish the work we are in — to bind up the nation's wounds — to care for him who shall have borne the battle, and for his widow and his orphan; and to do all which may achieve and cherish a just and lasting peace among ourselves and with the nations." — Abraham Lincoln

Someone has said: "For a man's words to carry any weight, the man himself must weigh at least a ton."

Jesus emphasized that great professions must be backed up with great deeds:

"Not every one that saith unto me, Lord, Lord shall enter into the kingdom of heaven; but he that doeth the will of my Father which is in heaven" (Matt. 7:21).


## 14. True Colors

One of the most interesting features of an operating room in a modern hospital is the lighting. This was demonstrated to me recently as my friend J. A. Gilbreath, administrator of Arkansas Baptist Hospital, took me on a tour of the hospital.

Engineers have used their skill and ingenuity to install the latest and best lighting facilities. The rooms can be flooded with fluorescent illumination. Not only is the lighting the best in quality, but it comes at such angles that the surgeon's hands never cast the slightest shadow as he performs his delicate services.

But, for one purpose in the operating room, the latest lighting is not the best. In one lamp, focused on the patient's face, is an incandescent bulb, old-fashioned in comparison with the lighting all around it. For this, as none of the bright lights, reflects the true color of the patient's face.

Because the slightest change in the patient's physical well-being during an operation is reflected in his color, the surgical team keeps careful watch. Often the warning first detected in the patient's change of color signals emergency attention which saves the patient's life.

What is your true color? As the incandescent lamp reveals the bodily color there are other "lamps" that show our true color as to the quality of our lives.

One of these is the revealing light of our loyalties. How loyal are we and to what? How consistently are we actually what we want the world to believe we are? Are we mere pretenders? How genuine are we, really? Any off color here indicates the desperate need for a Physician — for Christ, the Great Physician.


## 15. "Under New Management"

"Open to the Public Under New Management."

This is the sign exhibited prominently on the front of an eating place in our city. Although there is nothing here that would give the previous manager or managers legal grounds for a suit on defamation of character, there are some rather interesting implications. The most pointed implication is that "there have been some changes made" and not only are "things going to be different now," but these changes are going to be for the best interest of the public.

If you ponder this sign still further there are some questions that come naturally to your mind. You wonder not only what sort of fellow the previous manager was, but how open was his place and his operation to the public?

But so much for that.

For all practical purposes, when a person repents of his sins and trusts Christ as Lord and Savior he takes upon himself, in the baptismal service, something very much like this restaurant sign. "Open to the Public under New Management" shouts his public profession of faith and baptism.

Whatever one may have been in his heart, the fountain of his life, there is a remarkable change that comes about when he surrenders the reins of his life to the hands of Christ. Our sins are as scarlet, but "the blood of Jesus Christ . . . cleanses us from all sin."

This is not to say that the Christian is perfect or that he can, in the body of flesh, live above sin. But his whole outlook, his motivation of life, the desires of his heart all are changed. He will not abide in sin. Now he has come into unlimited resources for abundant living — the resources of God's unfathomable love and immeasurable power.

It is true of the new Christian's life, as the sign declares it to be of the restaurant under new management, that his life is "open to the public." The Christian, whatever else he may be, is ". . . the epistle of Christ. . . . Written not with ink, but with the Spirit of the living God; not in tables of stone, but in fleshy tables of the heart." And this epistle is "known and read of all men."

Yes, as Christians, we are open to the public under new management" — in our homes, at school, in our business relations, at the polls, at play, as well as at church.


## 16. "Give Me a Light"

Driving your car at night by the light of somebody else's car would not be a procedure recommended by the Safety Council or the Highway Patrol. Not even if the moon is shining so brightly that you can easily see the white dividing line as you trail a lighted car. But this was an interesting, if distasteful experience of mine on a recent Sunday night as I drove after church from Bentonville to Russellville.

The green light on the dashboard of my Renault came on a few miles north of Alma, indicating that the generator was no longer performing its function of recharging the car battery. My watch indicated the time to be a few minutes short of eleven. What a time to have the generator go out!

A stop at a service station confirmed my fears. The generator was dead and there was no way to do a repair job before the next day. Still an hour and a half's drive from my destination, I decided to try it. Maybe the battery could live that long. If not, I'd take my chances on finding a motel before my lights went out completely.

Then I conceived the notion of traveling by somebody else's lights. Never before had I been so conscious of the multiplicity of hills and hollows and curves that constitute so much of Highway 64 from Alma to Russellville. On straight stretches of road I found I could drive full speed ahead without using my lights by keeping my eyes on the center stripe and the car ahead, with a frequent glance into my rear-view mirror for any approaching traffic.

It worked. Not only did I make it to Russellville, but there was sufficient "juice" left in the old buggy for me to start it for the drive on to Little Rock the next day.

Driving by somebody else's light is a mighty poor substitute for driving by your own lights. But I am persuaded that many are traveling through life that way without realizing it.

How many are directed wholly or almost so by the "light" of somebody else's influence — "light" that may be the darkness of prejudice, hatred, ignorance! There is not much thinking today on our part as individuals. After all, thinking takes time and energy, and we have already drawn mighty heavily on both of these.

In our age of conformity, when the scarlet "sin" is that

of being different, the only safe light is Jesus Christ, the
Light of the world. He lights the hearts of all true followers.

## 17. Knowing about God

"When I am five I will know all about God."
So declared the four-year-old daughter of a preacher, with
all confidence.

"And the sad thing about it is that my daughter will
probably know more about God when she is five than when
she is 25," mused the father, as he reported the incident,
in a radio sermon the other day.

The kind of education our young people receive today
in our schools and colleges is too often that which causes
them to forget the things they knew about God in their
childhood years, rather than help them to know more about
God, the preacher continued. By the time young people
have completed their formal education and are entering upon
their careers, he said, they often have become so conformed
to the materialistic way of life so common in America today
that God and spiritual verities seem far away.

It is easy to make the schools the whipping boy, for that
implies that our homes and our churches, the other two of
the trio of character building institutions, are not failing
in their part of the responsibility.

Yet, for some reason or reasons, our homes have a harder
time influencing the young people to want to go to church
and our churches have a more difficult time enlisting and
keeping enlisted this age group than any other category.
Why?

The physical and material world is so attractive to young
people growing up that it is easy for them to be so happy
with what it has to offer that they lose sight of the spiritual
realm with its abiding verities and values. The danger of
taking Romans 12:2 in reverse and being conformed "to
this world" is greater for our young people than for anybody
else.

In our time, with the major emphasis so often on "having a good time" and the most temptations in the path of youth that we have ever had, it is easy to see why God becomes to many a long-bearded old man, who, even as did aged Isaac, sits away off somewhere in blindness, impotence, and decrepitude, far removed from the arena of daily lives.

The reason many, regardless of age, know so little about God is not that God is not near or that he cannot be known, but that he is to be known only by those who diligently seek him (Deut. 4:29).

## 18. Ancient Questions Still Haunting Us

One of the earliest of man's recorded questions, "Am I my brother's keeper?" with its related query, "Who is my neighbor?" reverberate across the skies of man's habitation today with a crescendo that drowns out the din of atomic blasts. How much territory, how much time did the Lord cover when he said: "Love one another"? Can we be disciples of Christ and restrict our love to ourselves? To our own families? To our own churches and denominations? To our own clubs and societies? To those of our own neighborhoods? To our own political parties? To our own nationalities? To our own races?

Can we cover all of these with our Christian affection and go on building interminable walls that shut out of our compassion others — others made to be in the image of God? Others for whom Christ died?

What does it mean to love our neighbors? Does it mean to love them reservedly? Does it have any practical application that reaches down to capital-labor relations? Does it concern itself with salaries and wages paid, with working conditions? Does it have any bearing upon the quantity and quality of labor a workman expends for his day's pay?

Does the love Christ commands of Christians have anything to do with race relations? With how we feel about people whose skins and whose languages and backgrounds may be quite different from our own?

Does the love we are to have as followers of Christ have anything to do with attitudes of our hearts toward our fellow men, whether in our judgment they are wise or foolish, rich or poor, good or bad?

Does the love of Christ in our hearts make any difference in the way we treat people, whoever they are and wherever they are, whether in the face-to-face relationships of living together in the home, or working together, doing business together, or just living in the same world?

Selfishness and self-centeredness, the very base of man's inhumanity to his fellow man, are narrow in their concepts and in their outlooks, but they are almost limitless in the scope of their influence for strife in our civilization. Here is the cancer that eats away at the vitals of our society today. And many of the remedies that are being hawked as sure-cures are pure and simple nostrums.

There is but one remedy that can kill this cancer and give man the health and vatality to love God with all his heart, with all his soul, with all his mind, and with all his strength, and to love his neighbors (all men everywhere) as himself. That is the regenerating love of Christ in the heart. But many who say they have the remedy still have all of the outward symptoms of fatal affliction.

Christ can be the Great Physician only to those who open their hearts to the healing balm of his redeeming love.

## 19. High Cost of Greed

> *How quickly Nature falls into revolt*
> *When gold becomes her object.*
> — King Henry

In one of the old school readers — was it McGuffey? — is the story of a greedy dog.

One day the dog was walking across a footlog with a

tasty bone in his mouth. Looking into the stream that flowed beneath the footlog and seeing his own reflection, he thought he was seeing another dog carrying a bone in its mouth.

"I'll take his bone and then I'll have two," thought the dog.

With a fierce growl he lunged at the other dog. But as he opened his mouth, he lost his own bone and a moment later he was struggling to save himself from drowning in the cold waters of the stream.

Greed is excessive hunger for something, the dictionary says — for food, as in the case of the man who sold his birthright for a mess of pottage; for wealth, as portrayed so vividly by Jesus in his account which begins: "The ground of a certain rich man brought forth plentifully. . . ." Greed also may be seen in an unquenchable longing for recognition, for fame, and the like.

Aesop tells of two neighbors, one of whom was avaricious and the other, envious. Appearing before Jupiter, who knew of their sins and was determined to let them punish themselves, they were told each could have whatever he wished for himself on one condition. Whatever one of them asked for himself he would receive, but the other would receive double of the same thing.

The avaricious man asked for a room full of gold. Promptly his request was granted. And he was happier than he had ever been until he discovered that his companion now had two rooms full of gold.

Then it came the turn of the envious man, who could not bear the thought of his neighbor having any joy at all. He promptly asked that one of his own eyes be put out, thus being assured that his companion would become totally blind.

The moral Aesop draws is that "sin brings its own punishment."

Jesus asks the soul-searching question: ". . . what is a man profited, if he shall gain the whole world and lose his own soul? or what shall a man give in exchange for his soul?" (Matt. 16:26).

## 20. The Seeing Eye

For a long time now I have been high-hatting some of my closest friends on the street. Time after time, one of them has slapped me on the back or hollered at me to let me know I had stared unseeingly in his direction.

It finally dawned on me that my three-year-old specs were probably needing to be stepped up. Sure enough, when I finally got around to seeing an eye doctor, that proved to be the case.

Nobody likes to be high-hatted. And not many would want to be a high-hatter. But you can't respond to friends and situations you do not know are there.

There are many dangers to your physical wellbeing when you can't see — especially in this age of the over-stuffed traffic lanes. But there's something far worse than physical blindness. Yes, spiritual blindness.

Jesus referred to a people whose "heart is waxed gross, and their ears are dull of hearing, and their eyes they have closed; lest at any time they should see with their eyes, and hear with their ears, and should understand with their heart, and should be converted, and I should heal them" (Matt. 13:15).

To those who came to him desiring to be made spiritually whole, Jesus said: ". . . blessed are your eyes, for they see: and your ears, for they hear. For verily I say unto you, That many prophets and righteous men have desired to see those things which ye see, and have not seen them; and to hear those things which ye hear, and have not heard them" (Matt. 13:16, 17).

Do you remember the sad story that broke in the newspapers a few months ago, about the disillusioned, 19-year-old girl who willed her eyes to a sightless person in a suicide note, saying: "I hope you'll be able to see more through them than I could"?

Regardless of the state of our physical eyes, there is much

that is marvelous to be seen in this life, for those whose hearts "hunger and thirst after righteousness."

If we could only have our spiritual insight sharpened as simply as getting a new pair of bi-focals for our physical sight! Or can we not?

## 21. "Fullness of time"

You don't travel far without running into an occasional roadblock. Using the term figuratively, that happens even if you are flying.

Recently I spent a full day going to Memphis from Little Rock and back, with many long hours of uncertainty in between in the Memphis airport.

My ticket had listed Memphis merely as the first stop — twenty-eight minutes from Little Rock — on what was to be a trip to Washington, D.C., with a day's stopover in South Carolina. But after sitting for two hours on a grounded jet on which I had hoped to travel from Memphis to Atlanta, the second leg of the trip, I learned that Atlanta was hopelessly fogged in. So I climbed off, claimed my luggage, and began trying to get passage back to Little Rock.

The plane on which I was eventually ticketed for the back-home flight normally would have left Memphis for Little Rock at 2 P.M. That day it ran exactly four hours late.

Originally, I had planned to leave Little Rock on a direct flight for Washington, leaving on Sunday. Then I had received a letter from the pastor of a South Carolina church where I had been the first pastor. The church was having its tenth anniversary services that Sunday morning and wanted me to participate.

Thrilled, I had changed my plans to leave a day early and go a little out of the way for the special engagement. But what had seemed a happy coincidence was not to be. We had worked out my schedule to the last detail, but the fog said no!

Two days later I got to make that trip to Washington. I missed seeing my South Carolina friends and helping them to celebrate, but I enjoyed those extra days at home. And that delayed trip turned out to be smooth sailing all the way.

In life, most people get grounded occasionally. And often the thing that grounds one is something beyond his control. The fog that grounds may not be a fog at all. It may be a great personal loss — in business, in love, in unattained goals — bringing disappointment, frustration, and sorrow. The one without both faith and patience is poor indeed.

So we pray: "Lord, thy will be done. You can see all the way. Ground us when that's best, and let us go on at your good pleasure, for we remember it was in the fullness of time that you came to our world. When we run into roadblocks, help us to see that even these fit into thy purpose for us."

## 22. A Required Course

Most of us come with grudge-nursers built in. Forgivers are extra equipment that has to be installed.

Forgiving does not come easy. There is nothing in our human natures that makes us want to forgive. And one reason it is so hard for us to forgive is that there is at least one thing that's even harder for us than forgiving — that's confessing our own shortcomings and asking to be forgiven.

But the Lord shows us that repenting and forgiving are required of every one who expects to be his disciple. In the Model Prayer, he teaches us to pray: ". . . forgive us our debts as we have forgiven our debtors" (Matt. 6:12).

At the conclusion of his story about the slave who had been forgiven his huge debt but who would show no mercy to a fellow slave who owed him a few dollars, Jesus said:

"And the master was enraged and turned him over to the official torturers, until he should pay the whole debt. This is the way my heavenly Father too will deal with you, if you do not, each one, heartily forgive your brother" (Matt. 18:34-35).

The Lord let his disciples know that the sky is the limit on how many times we are to forgive those who wrong us and then repent and ask forgiveness:

"Be always looking out for one another," the Lord said, in Luke 17:3-4. "If your brother ever sins, reprove him, and if he repents, forgive him. Even if he sins against you seven times in a day and seven times turns to you and says, 'I am sorry,' you must forgive him."

But when Peter seemed to get the idea that the Lord was setting a limit and giving a specific formula for forgiving, and asked how many times one must forgive — seven times in a day? — the Lord replied: "I tell you, not as many as seven, but as many as seventy times seven!"

It is humanly and divinely impossible to forgive someone who does not desire to be forgiven. The father of the prodigal son (Luke 15) yearned after his son all the time the youth was away in the far country of licentious living, but he could not forgive the young man until the son came to himself and turned back to his father in repentance.

So it seems that repenting and forgiving are heads and tails of the same coin. We cannot have one without the other. Men and women must forgive one another as they expect God to forgive them.

## 23. "What'm I bid?"

Back in December I dropped in on a Rotary club in a city of the deep south to make up my Little Rock Rotary attendance and found the club holding its annual auction sale for the benefit of a Crippled Children's hospital. Although the club was fairly small, having a membership of about 60 or 70, the sale's goal for the day was $2,000.

Various business firms of the city had co-operated, donating items to be auctioned. All of these, with one exception, had been packaged and gift-wrapped and were being auctioned as unknown quantities. The lone exception was a leather-bound Bible, King James Version, which had nothing but a red ribbon tied around it.

After the sale had been going on for some time and a number of packages — big ones and little ones — had been sold, always to the highest bidders, a preacher member of the club was called on to auction off the Bible.

"I'm not much of an auctioneer," the preacher said, "but you know what a good buy this book is. It'll do anybody good who'll read it. What am I bid?

"Twenty dollars," someone hollered.

"Twenty dollars, who'll make it forty?" challenged the preacher.

"Forty!" chimed somebody.

"Forty dollars, what do I hear?" said the auctioneer. "Here's a book that combines both the old and the new, going for forty dollars!"

With coaxing, the preacher got the bid up to $130, where it stood.

"$130 once! $130 twice! $130 three times, and sold!" barked the auctioneer. And the high bidder turned out to be a Rotarian of the Jewish faith.

Paying for the Bible, the Hebrew chided the Christians: "The Old Testament is worth that much!"

I could not help wondering how the sale of that Bible would have gone if no one in that group had owned or had access already to the Bible. Or if the only place they could read the Scriptures had been from a copy chained in a church, as was the situation in Europe during the Middle Ages.

The Bible is the greatest book, or collection of books, in the world, we say. Yet, to many Americans, it is not worth the paper and the ink to print it. For they have neither the time nor the inclination to read it, let alone heed it.

"Thy word have I hid in my heart" [not on a shelf] the Psalmist cries.

How much is the Bible worth to you?

## 24. Out of the Heart

Someone has said: "All of us want to be known and loved; but many are afraid to be known, lest they not be loved."

It will be an embarrassing day if the time ever comes when we can read one another's thoughts and intents. There is much pretending, at the best. You and I want to be known favorably to our associates and friends. So we try to cover up anything about ourselves that we feel would not be complimentary to us. And who, looking into the inner recesses of his heart, does not find much that disturbs him?

But it is often the little things that betray us to others for what we are. Fiction writers learn this. If an author wants to get across the idea that one of his characters is a heel, he doesn't say this in so many words. Instead, he lets you see the fellow kick a dog or drive out of his way to run over a cat, or knock a little child down. Of course, the reverse is true. It is little things that show the greatness of a person, such as going out of the way to do a kind deed to one who is mean and unloveable.

You can tell a great deal about a person if you know what he is like in even a small segment of his average, run-of-the-mill day. What is he like with the people where he works? If he is the boss, how does he treat those under him? How is he esteemed by his associates?

You can know a great deal about a person if you can find out how he spends his leisure. Where does he go, what does he do? Who are his friends? What does he read? What kind of movies or television programs does he like?

The secret of the good life is the condition of a person's heart. For one to make people think he is a kindly, compassionate person when, actually, he hates people except for what they can mean to him personally, is to live a lie. A wise man long ago proclaimed a great truth when he said: "Out of the heart come the issues of life."

What we need today is not so much better conduct as purer hearts. To try to make our conduct good when our hearts are bad is like tying fruit onto the limbs of a dead fruit tree to make the tree fruitful.

## 25. Even in Orbit

One of the big questions not even the 17 flights around the world by Russian cosmonaut Gherman S. Titov answers is what would be the effect of exposure to the weird condition of weightlessness for periods much longer than the twenty-five hours he was in orbit?

If space travel, with its accompanying weightlessness, gets to be the accepted thing, surely the dieting industry is going to be left high and dry. Then, instead of taking Metrecal or going on a rabbit diet, a plump matron or hefty consort could just climb aboard a rocket ship and in nothing flat go from two hundred forty pounds to zero.

For awhile there would be other angles on "weightlessness." Just think what a scramble there would be for orbital flights to get a few hundred miles away from the earth while the Legislature was in session; or around the first of the month when bills are piling up; or when the nerves are getting on edge from the monotonous turn of events at the office.

Wouldn't it be a joy to leave a sign on the door telling the milkman you will not need any milk for awhile, as you have gone to the moon? Or just to clear out and not tell even your next-door neighbor that you have gone to Mars?

But sooner or later many of the get-away-from-it-all advantages would surely peter out. The first thing you knew you would discover that your seatmate on the space ship was a neighbor who had hoped to get away from you for awhile, or, perhaps, a member of Congress on an expense account. Imagine your chagrin at discovering, just after your rocket has gone into orbit, that your mother-in-law is aboard, or Uncle Herman, or . . . .

But joking aside, there are not likely to be any weights you elude while in orbit that will not come crashing back upon you when you set back to terra firma. You may get away from the scene of some of your heartaches for awhile, but not even an orbital flight will mend a broken heart. The same trouble Mark Twain had on his trip to Europe will be yours — wherever you go, there will still be you, with all your personal problems.

Here is a sobering thought even for the new space age: each one of us will continue to be accountable to God, maker and sustainer of the universe:

"So then each one of us shall give account of himself to God" (Rom. 14:12).

## 26. "It Sure Is Funny . . ."

It sure is funny — on a plane and just settin' here on the ground!"

The little lad who said this was sitting with his mother and younger brother in a Central Airlines plane at Fort Smith, waiting for the take-off. Obviously he was quite thrilled as he looked forward to his first plane ride.

He had been doing most of his family's talking for several minutes as he took in every foot of the interesting interior of the plane and as he peeped out a window from time to time to see what the world looked like from an airplane.

But for some reason the take-off was delayed, or, at least, it did not come as soon as Junior had hoped and expected.

Then the humor and irony of the situation had broken upon him.

Here he was, aboard this great man-made bird that had wings and power to make it fly far above the world he had known up till now, and the plane was just sitting there, still on the ground. So far, being in a plane was little different from being inside a cotton wagon, peeping through the sideboards!

Presently the pilot and co-pilot came inside, closing the door which had opened to the outside world. The hostess checked to see that all safety belts were fastened, against the background of the "No Smoking" sign, and soon the plane was soaring far above the countryside, bound for Hot Springs.

The words of the boy still flash across my memory from time to time: "It sure is funny — on a plane and just settin' here on the ground!"

When I consider how God has blessed America and how many opportunities all of us have for self-improvement and for helping others, it sometimes occurs to me: "It sure is funny — having all these blessings and so many of us being ungrateful and self-centered!"

When I think what a blessing family life is — or could be — sometimes I muse: "It sure is funny — families have such nice places to live and they could have so much fun together as families, but they are divided up and gone their several ways to somewhere else most of the time!"

And somtimes at church, especially on Sunday and Wednesday nights, I catch myself thinking: "It sure is funny — we live in a land of religious liberty and have such beautiful and comfortable places to worship, and worship can mean so much to a Christian, and yet so many of our pews are seldom used!"

## 27. Two-way Traffic

Driving your car on the superhighways that are being constructed across the country is delightful. You don't have to worry about stop lights, or traffic cutting in or out from outside streets and roads. And if there's somebody in front of you who doesn't want to drive as fast as the law allows, you can usually go around him.

Yes, you can just hold your foot on the accelerator at the clip you want and breeze right along, with your conscience — and police radar — as your guide.

But it's rather frustrating, after you have been cruising along at 65 to 70 miles an hour long enough to just about be used to having the road all to yourself, to come to one of those jarring signs that lets you know you are about to come back to earth and to two-way traffic.

This happened to me the other day as I was zooming north on the superhighway now in use from Little Rock to a point above Jacksonville. Suddenly there was the sign: "Two-way traffic."

Brother, I had to do some adjusting quick! And as I ran out of the superhighway onto just the ordinary highway, there was a fellow in front of me in a pick-up truck, just moseying along. On the new road it had been against the law to travel less than 45 and you could legally go 70. But on the old road there was no minimum and the maximum was 60. What a come-down!

As I have had time to meditate and philosophize a little, I wonder, really, if we Americans are spiritually ready for the great network of coast-to-coast freeways (a farmer friend of mine calls them "free-for-alls") that are being built and which will soon become commonplace. You can get to be mighty self-satisfied and self-centered on superhighways. If a fellow is not careful, he'll just about get to feeling that the road is his personal, private property and nobody else has any rights but him.

A lot of trouble we have, spiritually, is in going our own

ways, under our own stream, so to speak, with the old attitude: "The devil take the hindmost." It is hard for us to realize sometimes that the road of life is and always must be a two-way thoroughfare that brings us into direct contact with fellow travelers.

The roads our Savior walked were not superhighways. They were the common, two-way roads, often dirty and crowded with care-worn travelers. He calls Christians to follow him as burden bearers in the stream of humankind.

## 28. The Slowpokes

The State of Arkansas recently got out a pamphlet dealing with a class of drivers on the streets and highways — the slowpoke. The pamphlet was to be given out with the new drivers' licenses. They sent me one early, for some reason!

For the driver who has somewhere to go, there are few things more frustrating than to have the road blocked by a slowpoke. And the longer one has to stay in line behind the 'poke, the more his dander rises. Sometimes the traffic will be slowed to a cold-molasses drip for a mile by a driver who barely creeps along and seems to have no conscience on what he is doing with the rights of others to the use of the road.

Even worse than the slowpoke — who after all, is moving, if slowly — is the driver who does not hesitate to stop his car dead still in the line of traffic, often without warning, to let someone get out or in, instead of pulling off the road for the stop.

Then there is the fellow who doesn't know where he is going and who stops at least briefly at every intersection — and then spurts ahead just as you are getting ready to go around him.

They might not be the same people, but you also run into the snails, the stoppers and the hesitators in the drivers' seats in business, the church, the school, and elsewhere in society.

How can a fellow lead if he is not going anywhere, or if he doesn't know where he is going? Yet, there are an abundance of people, it seems, who aspire to nothing more than the honor that goes with an office. Once they have been elected, they have arrived.

The more strategic the place, the more likely the "leader" is to be run over or passed up. That's why it is so difficult for one who is lazy or inept to last in the pastorate. For the pastorate is probably the most difficult place to fill in the church, except, of course, the presidency of a Christian college.

"Amen! and amen!" you are saying. For you think this columnist is talking just about your preacher, or your mayor, or your children's teacher over at the public school.

Wrong again, brother, sister. I'm talking about you — and me. For each one of us Christians is in a very strategic driver's seat. And if we are not careful we can be getting in somebody else's way to the abundant life. Let's not be slowpokes on life's highway.


## 29. Church Termites

A lady connected with a termite eradication firm called us the other day to see if we'd be interested in carrying a news story on how to get rid of termites. When we explained to her that we could not use the story, since there was no religious connection, and ours is a religious publication, she dealt us an uppercut: "Hum-m-mh!" she replied, "I've seen stuff in there that wasn't very religious!"

As we have thought more about it and have read up a little on the habits of termites, we have decided that there might be a lot of pastors and other church leaders who would be interested in tips on how to get rid of "termites."

Occasionally when one pastor has wandered over into

another pastor's territory in quest of more sheep for his own
flock, the other pastor has been heard to suggest: "I've got
a hundred I'll be glad to give you, if you will let me pick
them!"

A termite, whether he's of the subterranean tribe or belongs
to one of the other two groups common to the United States
— damp-wood or dry-wood variety — according to the ency-
clopedias, "stands near the bottom of the scale of insect life."

And he's near the bottom in his self-centered bent for
taking care of old No. 1 and his voracious appetite, even
if it means causing your house to fall in on you, or you to
fall through your house.

A termite is about as sneaking and underhanded as any
member of insect society. He seeks darkness rather than
light. He will hide away to do his dirty work of undermining
on whatever he latches himself, and he will have a lot of
his destructive work accomplished before anybody but his
own termite buddies knows what's going on.

Termites have awfully soft shells, and so they are easy
to get their feelings hurt, but they are mighty hard to be
rid of. Nothing short of a small chemical war will dislodge
them from what they are feeding on. (Unfortunately, this
method of eradication is "out of bounds" in dealing with
church "termites.")

We believe the application is clear. Certainly church
members who hang onto the church for what it means to
them but who mean nothing but trouble and hindrance to the
church, are a lot like the termite. So, certainly, are the
sneakers who are always going stealthily about trying to
create a stink or disturbance.

Being sure the church is built of "living stones" is the
surest safeguard against "termites."

## 30. Shining Lights

Christ says of Christians that we are the light of the world.

Now there is light that comes directly from the sun and there is light that comes indirectly from the sun by way of the moon — reflected light. The Greek New Testament makes it clear that Christ is not speaking in this instance of a reflected light, but of a direct light. He has made us to be lights of the same type and nature as himself.

Without Christians the world with all of its gay whiteways would have no spiritual light. Without Christians a darkness would enshroud the world so dense it could be felt.

Christ himself is the light that "lighteth every man that cometh into the world." But it is his plan for Christians to light the world. This reveals the tragedy of backslidden Christians and hypocrites who "having a form of godliness, deny the power thereof."

Some of my readers will remember what a hard time we used to have trying to keep the wicks of the old No. 2 coal oil lamps trimmed and their chimneys clean so that we could have enough of their feeble rays to find our way around before we started running everything but our wives by electricity.

The amount of light we could expect from even a coal oil lamp (sometimes called "hayburner") depended to some extent upon the size of the lamp. A No. 2 was bigger and better than a No. 1.

The energy of the lamp was also important. If the oil supply were allowed to get low, the light would grow dim — or, to be more accurate, more dim. And if the oil were not kept replenished the light would burn out. The position of the lamp and the cleanness of its chimney, as already suggested, were important factors in the lighting of a room.

As the light of the world, Christians must be concerned about their size, individually and in the aggregate. Through spiritual nurture we can grow daily. We must have the oil

of the Holy Spirit abiding within us and we need constantly
to keep the chimneys of our lives unspotted from the world.

"Let the lower lights be burning! Send a gleam across
the wave! Some poor fainting, struggling seaman you may
rescue, you may save."

## 31. "Whom Say Ye . . . ?"

"Our church would have to close shop if it weren't for
the women."

So spoke a layman to me in a church I visited recently.

No doubt it is true that many of our churches are largely
"run" by women. Not that the women would have it that
way, but they must often stand in the breach because there
just aren't any men around.

It may be a business man spoke for many other men
when he said to me quite frankly: "I would be a good church
member if 'they' [meaning his church] would just leave
me alone! I stopped going to Sunday school just to keep
from being loaded with a lot of jobs I didn't have time to do."

Is loyalty to the church optional for men? Are we to go
and participate only if it does not interfere with our own
plans, our own business, our own way of life? Or is loyalty
to the church a royal command from the one we have
professed to be the Lord of our lives and who has himself
become "head of the corner"?

Is the church just another competitor for our time, along
with the lodge, the civic club, the business, the recreational
interests? Or is the church a working organization of re-
deemed men and women the purpose of which is to get
the sin remedy of the gospel out to a lost and dying world?

At a stage of his ministry when it had become popular to
follow him, Jesus said to a multitudinous congregation:
". . . whosoever doth not bear his cross, and come after
me, cannot be my disciple."

We may have to decide just how important the church is.

And that cannot be settled without first answering the question of Christ, its founder, ". . . *whom say ye that I am?*"

## 32. A Chain's Strength

A chain is no stronger than its weakest link.

The truth of this old saying is being re-emphasized by two new submarine telephone cables recently laid from North America to Europe.

First under-ocean telephone lines to be laid, the two cables, each about 2,250 land miles long, stretch from Clarenville Newfoundland, to Port Lathaiche on the Firth near Oban, Scotland.

Built at a cost of $42,000,000, the submarine system already has doubled the number of overseas calls. And the cost of a three-minute, person-to-person call has dropped from $75 when radio telephone service opened in 1927 to $12 on week days and $9 on evenings and Sundays.

But each of the cables is only as lasting as its weakest tube. The engineers hope they will last at least twenty years. But the moment one tube "blows" an entire cable will be out. And it would probably be simpler to lay a whole, new cable than to find the defunct tube and replace it, the engineers report.

This has a lesson for us church members. Every one of us is important to the work of the church. Fortunately, a church does not have to close when one of its members quits. But no church is big enough or strong enough not to be hurt when one member becomes cold, indifferent, or worldly. The importance of every individual member to the life of the church is seen in Paul's classic statement:

*For as we have many members in one body, and all members have not the same office;*

*So we, being many, are one body in Christ, and every one members one of another (Rom. 12:4-5).*

It is amazing that our churches accomplish so much, with

only about fifty per cent of their members qualifying for
the designation of "active."

## 33. Fishing in a Tub

Ever hear of the man who decided to fish in a tub?

After months and years of going fishing every week or two,
he began to get lazy and stingy. He got to thinking how
tired he was after an afternoon at the lake, hooking up and
unhooking his boat, loading and unloading his motor, gasoline
can, tackle box, bait, poles, etc. One day he made the
fatal mistake of figuring up how much per pound the fish
he caught were costing him. That was the last straw. He
decided to fish in a tub in his back yard.

So when Thursday afternoon came — he always fished on
Thursdays so that he could be home for prayer meeting on
Wednesdays — he got a No. 2 washtub and set it out under
a shade tree in his back yard, got his fishing pole and line,
pulled up a comfortable lawn chair and he was "in business."

(I realize that in this gadget age a lot of the rising
generation are so ignorant of the finer things of life they
don't know what a No. 2 washtub is. When you say "tub"
these days a lot of folks think you are talking about a boat,
or a bathtub!)

Well, for a while our hero really enjoyed the new routine.
Fishing in a tub was so saving on the energies. No tugging
at boats, at motors — or at fish! It was not even necessary
to stay awake, for when you fish in a tub you'll catch as
much asleep as awake. And it was so economical! He saved
all his bait bill, for when you fish in a tub you catch as
many without bait as with it. And a lot of days he caught
as much fishing in the tub as he had caught many a day
when he had fished from his boat in his favorite lake.

But it was not all roses. He no longer thrilled as Thursday
afternoon approached. And, fishing in his tub, he missed
the thrill of seeing his cork disappear and feeling the tug

of a big bream, crappie, catfish or bass on the end of his line. He could no longer tell about the big ones that got away. It finally dawned on him that saving energy and money is not so hot when you never catch any fish!

Christians who determine their daily lives on the basis of what is easy, what requires little or no exertion and costs nothing, are like the man who fished in a tub.

And churches made up of such members are not doing any better.

"Come," said Jesus to some fishermen long ago, "follow me, and I will make you fishers of men!"

## 34. Absent in Spirit

Not all who go to church go there to worship. I know for I have been guilty myself.

And this considerably less than a thousand years ago. It was brought home to me on a recent Sunday when, with no place to preach that day, I sat with the congregation in my home church.

The offering had just been taken and the organist was playing something before the special music preceding the sermon. Suddenly it dawned on me that I was present in body but, at least for the time being, absent in spirit. I was just sitting and waiting for the pastor to take the pulpit. And while waiting, my mind was several country miles away.

The silent witness of a mother at prayer, on a pew two or three seats ahead of me, reminded me that I was in a place of worship. The organ music was obviously more than a fill-in for her. She sat with head bowed and eyes closed. Ashamed, I called my mind back to my body and took note of the fact that the organ was playing one of the great hymns, a prayer itself. Its words came fresh to my heart:

*Jesus, keep me near the cross,*
*There a precious fountain*
*Free to all — a healing stream,*
*Flows from Calv'ry's mountain.*
*In the cross, in the cross,*
*Be my glory ever;*
*Till my raptured soul shall find*
*Rest beyond the river.*

We preachers sometimes joke about the absentees who are "present in spirit but not in body." But to be present in body but not in spirit is not worth much to the split personality or to the spirit of the service itself. Again, I know whereof I speak. I was there. For one thing, you certainly are not going to be praying if your mind is wandering, or if it is full of a thousand things far removed from the attitude of worship. Without prayer and meditation there cannot be worship. And when we rob ourselves of the experience of worship we cheat ourselves of that which we can least afford to be without.

If we are to worship, we must discipline our minds and our hearts. The organ and piano music, the singing by the choir and the congregation, the public and private prayers, the offering itself — all are or should be far more than "preliminaries." They are aids to worship itself. They help to prepare our hearts for the sermon.

For many of us who go to church, the sermon and the service may be worth little or nothing simply because we just sit and stand and never really tune our hearts in.


## 35. The Heart Warmer

A friend of mine who works for a used car dealer spends half his time starting cars that are not going anywhere. Every car on the lot must be started every day or two to keep the battery charged and the car in operating condition. But with the exception of an occasional sale or trial runs of cars being considered by customers, the vehicles continue to stand in their tracks on the display lot day after day. My friend showed one to me that has not been off the lot in nearly a year. But he has continued to start it and run the motor at regular and frequent intervals. There is always the hope and the possibility with each new day that somebody will buy it and put it on the road.

Pastors have a lot in common with the man on the used car lot. Thy spend a big part of their time and energy warming the hearts of church members who are not going anywhere as far as spiritual growth and service are concerned. A lot of us are quite content with the feeling of satisfaction that comes from being in church every Sunday or two and hearing a good sermon. But for the most part, the value of worship is purely subjective, for the greater part of the congregation will go out to live their lives the same old way and conduct their business as usual until they are back — next Sunday or a Sunday or two after that — for another heart-warming.

About half the members of a typical church do not even come out to get their hearts warmed. Religion has long since become for them a load instead of a lift. If they should be persuaded to come they would be bored by the service and would go away feeling that the time had been wasted. They have been withdrawn from God and his church so long that their hearts have become cold and indifferent and their consciences seared. Many of them no longer feel guilty about their backslidden condition. These are among the first to find fault with the church and to claim they are "as good" or "better" than those who still take their church responsibilities and opportunities seriously.

These are like the car with the dead battery and the motor corroded from lack of use.

But just as the occasional sale keeps the starter of cars on his job, the ever present prospect of seeing some member of his congregation begin living the Christian life abundantly keeps the preacher plugging away from week to week at the business of warming hearts.

## 36. Laws of Harvest

The Scriptures warn: "Be not deceived; God is not mocked: for whatsoever a man soweth, that shall he also reap" (Gal. 6:7).

What you sow, you reap. If you sow wild oats, do not expect to have a harvest of wheat.

Another law of the harvest is that there is a direct connection between how much you sow and the abundance of the harvest. The compiler of Proverbs puts it this way: "There is that scattereth, and yet increaseth; and there is that withholdeth more than is meet, but it tendeth to poverty" (Prov. 11:24).

You cannot be stingy with your sowing without cutting down on the harvest. How foolish the farmer would be who would say, "This seed is too good to waste in the fields. Let's eat it."

Many of our churches are not accomplishing much just because their pastors and deacons and people have their eyes and hearts closed to these laws of the harvest. All too little planting is being done. There are still a lot of people who feel their churches have had a good year if they have paid all their bills and have some money left.

Where in the Bible does it say the Lord is calling churches primarily to save money? He has called us to help save a lost world, regardless of the cost.

And not all of the cost can be dollars, however liberal we give of our tithes and offerings. The greatest thing that can be said of the giving or the sowing of any church was said by Paul about the Macedonian churches: ". . . in a severe test of affliction, their abundance of joy and their extreme poverty have overflowed in a wealth of liberality on their part . . . but first they gave themselves to the Lord and to us by the will of God."

According to the sowing will be the harvest.


## 37. To God Be the Glory

Many times in history the world has waited with bated breath to see if man in daring conquest could reach beyond a last border. But never before had so many millions watched by television so awe-inspiring an event as that of Feb. 20 which saw courageous Col. John H. Glenn, Jr., hurtled into space as the first American to travel around the world by satellite.

Unlike the Russians, in orbiting a man ahead of us, this blast-off was not kept secret. The whole world — the free world, that is — had been alerted and was standing by with Col. Glenn for the countdown.

I witnessed the historic event with Duke K. McCall, president of Southern Seminary, on the screen of a television set in a room at the Hermitage Hotel in Nashville, Tennessee. We were both silent in the minutes leading up to and during the blast-off. I am sure that Dr. McCall was praying, as I was, for the safety of our noble adventurer.

As I marvelled at what was happening before the eyes of so many millions of us, four words connected with another great experiment came to my mind: "What hath God wrought!"

Comparatively few people knew about it at the time, but those who did must have been breathless, on May 24, 1844, when the show-down came on a new-fangled invention called electro-magnet telegraph.

The inventor, Samuel Finley Breese Morse, had campaigned for years for funds to erect a test line. Finally, he had persuaded Congress to appropriate $30,000 for the construction of a 40-mile line from Washington, D.C. to Baltimore. The first message to go out, upon the success of which so much depended, was sent by Morse from the Supreme Court Room at the nation's capitol and was received instantly in Baltimore: "What hath God wrought!"

What better words are there to summarize the latest achievement? God has used a stalwart Christian man to bear a unique testimony to the world and to expand our horizons.

To God be the glory in the Space Age as in every age!


## 38. Strings Attached

Three things Calvary Baptist Church in down-town Washington, D. C., must have in perpetuity — an organ, a bell, and a clock.

This was part of the bargain, many years ago, when Amos Kendall, a non-Christian, gave $90,000 for the construction of the church auditorium at the corner of 8th and H streets.

Mr. Kendall was a highly gifted person. The late President Woodrow Wilson said of him that those who would know the administration of President Andrew Jackson must know Kendall, who wrote Mr. Jackson's official papers.

Pastor Cranford, in a devotional welcome recently to Baptists attending the Third Annual Conference on Religious Liberty, sponsored by the Baptist Joint Committee on Public Affairs and held at Calvary Church, said of the organ, the bell and the clock:

"The organ reminds us that we need harmony in the world and in our hearts.

"The bell reminds us that we need to call the world back to God, if the world is to have harmony.

"The clock reminds us that we do not have forever to get on with our job."

But there was one string attached to the Kendall donation that was to backfire on the donor himself. That was a provision that the membership of the church should include as associate members any non-Christians who, as Mr. Kendall, gave to its support.

Many years later, a bereaved mother, a member of Calvary Church, called on Mr. Kendall and pointing an accusing finger at him, declared: "Our son has died without accepting Christ, and it is your fault. You are to blame for his being lost!"

Mr. Kendall was dumbfounded. "What do you mean? How can you say such a thing?" he asked.

The mother then related how that when she and her husband had tried to win their son to Christ he had declined to accept. "Mr. Kendall is a good man and he has never accepted Christ," he had said.

This crushed the now aging Mr. Kendall. Falling to his knees he repented of his sins and accepted Christ. On the first opportunity he presented himself for baptism.

He now became a great soul-winner. The first day he gave his personal testimony, twenty men stepped out to accept Christ as Savior. But it was too late for the lad who had made Mr. Kendall his model.

## 39. Earth-bound Geese

An old story, about the geese that never flew, was brought to mind again the other day as we read the latest epistle of "Simeon Stylites," Halford E. Luccock, in *The Christian Century*.

The fable, attributed by Dr. Luccock to the Danish theologian, is about a flock of geese that once lived together in a barnyard. Once a week they would come together in a corner of the yard, at which time one of the more eloquent ganders would mount the fence and hold forth in glowing terms on the wonders of geese.

He would recount the exploits of their forefathers who mounted on wing and flew the trackless sky. He would speak of the goodness of the Creator who had given geese the urge to migrate and wings with which to fly.

As he spoke, the geese would nod their heads and marvel at these things and remark to one another on the eloquence of the preaching goose. All this they did, with great unanimity. But one thing they never did, with equal unanimity — they did not fly. Each time they would go back to their waiting dinner, for the corn was good and their barnyard quite secure.

We do not know about their orthodoxy, but their orthopraxy would certainly square with our typical churches. They were playing church along with the best of us.

One day a little boy who had stayed for church in spite of the fact that his parents went home after Sunday school, had a wonderful experience during the worship service in which he felt God calling him to preach. Upon arriving home, after church, he found his mother very curious as to who was at church that day. Was Aunt Mary there? The boy did not know. What about Uncle John? The lad could not say whether Uncle John was there.

The mother asked about two or three other friends or relatives, with the same response. Finally, in desperation, she retorted: "I don't think you know whether anybody was at church!"

"Yes," replied the son, "God was there!"

If the experience of worship bounces off our lives like water off a duck's (or goose's) back, how much better are we than Kierkegaard's geese?


## 40. "Cheerful Helpfulness"

Want to be successful?

Then your main job is not to find someone who will help you, but find a way to be "cheerfully helpful" yourself.

That is the point of a feature carried some time ago in the *Columbus Dispatch.*

Learning to be "cheerfully helpful" is, according to the article, the first lesson in success and "ought to be learned early by every boy and girl." And the place to learn this lesson, the writer continues, is in the home, for if it is learned in the home, it "will be second nature everywhere else."

We note further:

"If the young folks will start out with the thought that the greatest thing in the world is serving others and not being served by them, all of the latter that anybody could wish will come as a natural result. Do you doubt it? Put the question to yourself, Whom do you like to serve?

"Invariably, the answer will be those who serve or are willing to serve you. Not the quarrelsome, petulant, bullying persons about you, but those who are cheerful, watchful and willing to do the little things that smooth the rough texture of everyday life.

"Those who soonest make a place for themselves in the home or in money-earning tasks are those who are quick to see what they can do to help and are willing to do it, giving time and effort to the task of learning, if it be difficult. It is thus that the office boy becomes a clerk, the clerk a partner in the business and the partner the head of the firm. And the same way up is open to the young woman in any part of the employment that she seeks.

"On the other hand, the sure way to failure is through blindness to the little bits of helpfulness, evasion of duty, watchfulness of the clock that not an extra minute of time may be put in; the expectation that, while you give ungrudging service to none, everybody will give it to you.

"Opportunity opens wide to the cheerful, helpful person, but her gates must be pried open for those who lack good will and expect always to be helped."

The writer might have said that the home is the best place to start because that is where we are with the people who are nearest and dearest to us. What better way to make home a little heaven on earth than through the practice of

such loving thoughtfulness by its members as here recommended? And where is the home that does not afford scores
of opportunities every day for each member of the family
to be "cheerfully helpful"?

## 41. The Smell of New Books

My liking for books dates back to my earliest recollection.
I liked books so well by the time I started to school that I
literally "ate up" a goodly part of my first First Reader. I
can still remember the flavor of the beloved McGuffey's
Readers.

There is something fascinating about a new book. The
smell of the fresh ink and paper is as welcome to the
olfactory nerves of the bookworm as the smell of honeysuckle
in the spring of the year or the aroma of burning cornstalks
on a frosty fall morning — something the younger generation
may not know about now that farmers have learned the
wisdom of plowing their stalks under instead of burning
them.

A love for books is a real asset to parents at this time
of the year when they are having to dig down into their
pockets and come up with enough to buy a new set for
each young'un they have in school above the sixth grade —
the State — or, rather, the taxpayers — pay for them in the
lower grades. If the parents get a kick out of leafing through
the school books this will help to assuage the sharp pains
in the pocket-book area.

I have just been looking over our daughter Judy's *English
in Action, Course* 4, by Tressler and Christ. It is encouraging
to find that the book not only includes grammar, composition,
rhetoric, and other items commonly found in English books,
but it also has something on "Personality and Human Relations," something I've been needing to read for a long time.

It is a pleasant surprise — religion has been so completely
divorced from public instruction — to find in the chapter

on getting along with people an essay by Joan Klinger, a high school student, in which she states:

". . . Religion must be part of our lives. We live at a high rate of speed partly because we have to and partly because we like it, but every day we should take time for the renewing of our faith in God and in humanity. We cannot separate our religion from our lives, our beliefs from our occupations, or our faith from our actions. . . . I have the utmost faith in the future of the world. Men are now moved . . . by the conception of a better state of society under which the rights of human beings will be recognized and a greater justice be done to all classes of humanity."

That's pretty good reading for high school seniors — and for their Dads and Mothers!


## 42. Watch the Oil

One of the best deals I ever made involved the use of a new, Model-T Ford. That was back when the Model-T was modern and you could get it in any color you wanted, if you wanted black.

It is eight miles from London to Russellville, site of the nearest high school at the time to which I refer, and I was to be a commuter to Russellville High each day. Sounds simple in this day when everybody has a car. But it was not so simple then, for I did not have so much as a bicycle.

Shortly before school was to start in the fall one of my former school teachers at London came to me with a proposition. He had a Model-T and a daughter who needed to get back and forth to school. If I would consent to drive the car, I could have my transportation free.

I never believed in rushing into anything without the most careful consideration. So I thought it all over, in half a second, and said I would do it.

That was a great year. Not the least of the highlights was dropping by the car owner's home each afternoon after putting the car up, and courting an older daughter, who, incidentally, has now been my dear wife for many years.

Something my unsuspecting and future father-in-law said to me the day he turned over to me the key to the Model-T has stayed with me: "Erwin, watch the oil," he said. "It won't run without gas. But you can be driving down the road thinking all is well, and you can be burning out the motor for lack of oil."

Watch the oil! What a parable of life. We will not run without three square meals a day — and, perhaps, refreshments between meals and at bedtime. But we can go right along without much thought of the need for the oil of spiritual nourishment and we can burn out our lives for lack of the things that really count.

If we meet all the material needs of ourselves and our families and even live in the finest homes and drive the longest, sleekest automobiles and provide the latest and biggest-screened TV's, and find no time nor place for Christ in our lives we are like the "certain rich man" Jesus tells about in Luke 12, whose ground "brought forth plentifully" but who is called "rich fool."

Watch the oil!


## 43. Poisonous Snakes

Two things I learned to fear early in life — snakes and tornadoes. I learned these fears from my nearest and best boyhood playmate, who had learned them from his father.

My friend could tell hair-raising tales about people who had been bitten by diamond rattlers or cotton-mouthed moccasins and had died on the spot. His stories kept me from breathing freely as we played in ditches, dammed branches, caught waterdogs, or entertained ourselves otherwise in the wide, open spaces.

And the fear of being blown away in a tornado kept me from getting the greatest enjoyment out of "staying all night" at the friend's home on many a summer night. I remember vividly the many occasions when I was awakened in the middle of sultry summer nights by the spine-tingling warning: "Get up, boys! Get up! It's coming up a storm!"

My friend is gone now. He has been dead for many years. His home was never struck by a tornado and as far as I know he never came close to being bitten by a poisonous snake. But he fell the victim of poison as deadly as the venom of a rattlesnake — a poison called alcohol.

The daddy, in teaching his son to keep a sharp lookout for snakes and storms, failed to impress upon him the dangers of taking a few drinks of liquor. A few drinks led to more and more and soon he had become a drunkard. One winter night he fell by the road in a drunken stupor and was not found until the next morning. Pneumonia, caused by the liquor and the exposure, cost him his life.

Many of our young people are growing up without fear of the poison of alcohol. Many of them see their parents and friends drink and serve it. The liquor industry wraps it in attractive packages and uses every means of making it appear to be desirable. Society has largely accepted it as a mark of hospitality. Our laws make it legal. But all of this makes it no safer than rattlesnakes sprayed with perfume and left to coil where our children play.

"*At the last it biteth like a serpent, and stingeth like an adder*" (Prov. 23:32).

## 44. Untarnished Crowns

There is something fascinating about a king's crown. One of the leading points of interest to the hundreds of thousands of people who visit Edinburgh (Scotland) Castle each year is the Crown Room where are displayed "The Honours of Scotland." Included in "The Honours" is the Crown, the Scepter and the Sword of State.

The Crown was remodelled in 1540 by order of James V.

It is made of Scottish gold and is decorated with 94 pearls, 10 diamonds and 33 other precious stones. The velvet cushion on which it rests is 300 years old.

The Scepter was presented to James IV by Pope Alexander VI in 1494 and was refashioned by James V. At the head of the gilded silver rod are figures of the Virgin Mary, James and Andrew, surmounted by a globe of rock crystal and a Scottish Pearl.

The Sword of State was given to James IV in 1507 by another Pope, Julius II, whose name is etched on the blade, together with etchings of Peter and Paul. Its wooden scabbard, covered with crimson silk, bears the Pope's arms on an enameled plate.

One of the most tragic of the royal persons to wear the Scottish Crown was Mary, Queen of Scots. When the Crown was placed on her little head and the Scepter thrust into her tiny hand, at the age of nine months, she cried. And well she might if she could have known what was ahead of her. She was to be the sixth Scottish ruler to die a tragic death.

Once, for a period of 111 years, the Honours were hidden away in a sturdy oak chest, from 1707 to 1818, because it was feared they would be taken to England. They were brought out largely on the efforts of Sir Walter Scott, after Royal permission was secured to open the chest.

The Honours were found, tarnished but undamaged. Today they glow in their original brillance.

In an earthly kingdom, there can be only one crown, for the ruling monarch. And even when it is made of the finest gold, it becomes tarnished and requires polishing. But in the Kingdom of God, there is a Crown of Life for every true believer in Christ. And this is a Crown that never becomes tarnished.


## 45. The Law of Christ

The other day I was trying to get across the Broadway

bridge to my domicile in North Little Rock. The time was 4:50 p.m. and the "5 o'clock shadow" of traffic fast becoming a reality. As usual, I was in the left lane of the north-bound traffic, for I have a left turn a block after leaving the bridge. This lane moves as fast, normally, as the right lane, for no left turns are allowed till you are across the bridge.

But I noticed that the stream in the right lane was moving off and leaving us. Several times we could not budge an inch on a change of the traffic light. The best we could do was to edge up about the length of a car.

After several minutes of this I saw a chance to swing over into the right lane and did so. I was able then to drive right on across. Not till I was three-fourths of the way across the bridge did I discover the reason for the block in the left lane. There, at the head of a solid mile of vehicles was a stalled car, occupied by a forlorn and helpless woman.

The south-bound traffic was a little lighter than the north-bound stream and once in a great while a north-bound driver was able to go around the stalled car on the left, pre-empting momentarily part of the bridge which is supposed to be the sole possession of south-bound traffic. So that was why we had been able to move at all.

Why in the world didn't some fellow give that woman a push? There are service stations and garages at the north end of the Broadway bridge. I wonder. Surely the fact she was very dark complexioned would not have made the difference. She was as desperately in need of help as if she had been the fairest blonde.

One thing was sure. Her trouble was the trouble of scores of others of us who happened to be in the same line of traffic. And all those who passed her by without giving her the help she needed were failing to help, not just one person, but scores.

That's the way it is with the human race. When one person gets stalled, there is a degree in which we are all stalled. And whatever we do to help one person, helps the human race. That's the way the Lord made us.

A long time before Scouting developed with its "Do a useful turn each day," Paul urged: "Bear ye one another's burdens, and so fulfill the law of Christ" (Gal. 6:2).

## 46. Secret of Living

A small group of Little Rockians meet each night for "coffee" at a downtown hotel. Senator John McClellan graces the group with his presence from time to time as he is stopping over in the city. One night recently, I am told, the Senator took note of the fact that one of the women in the party had brought along a current book on how to control tension.

"What are you doing reading a book like that?" asked the Senator.

"I have tensions," the woman confessed, with a smile.

"Can't you control your tensions?" he asked.

"No, and I thought this book might help me."

"Would you like to know what I've found most effective for tension?" asked Mr. McClellan.

"Yes," said the lady, possibly expecting that he would suggest some other book in the growing and prosperous field on how to face the daily frustrations of life.

"Prayer," replied the Senator.

Learning to live is a lot like learning to ride a bicycle. The sooner you can get your attention off yourself, the sooner you can expect to go zooming along in perfect balance.

You can't learn to ride a bike by merely reading a book. And neither can you learn to live a serene life by something you read. This may jar some of my readers, but reading a book is not sufficient — even if it be the Bible itself. How many have read the Bible, at least after a fashion, but have found no help.

The Bible is the Book of books. No other book is worthy to be compared with it. But it is not enough that the

Bible is a beacon light showing the way to God. One must walk in that light.

Want the secret of living from one of the world's great Christians? Here it is:

"Be careful for nothing; [don't worry] but in everything by prayer and supplication with thanksgiving let your requests be made known unto God. And the peace of God, which passeth all understanding, shall keep your hearts and minds through Christ Jesus" (Phil. 4:6-7).

## 47. Stopping All Leaks

You get so used to having hot water and plenty of it that you get to feeling, the way most of our homes are equipped these days, that it's unconstitutional not to have it. One young woman bewailed the fact that she didn't have a 40-gallon tank, instead of the customary 30. When asked why she and her husband and little girl needed the larger tank, she replied: "With a 30-gallon tank, if you do two washers of clothes, one right after the other, you have to wait several minutes before there's enough hot water to wash your hair!"

The sad news that fell upon my ears from my wife and daughter the other morning, just as I was thinking about getting up, was: "There's no hot water!"

That was the first time I had heard such ominous words in the five years we have been in our present domicile. Realizing that others who had occupied our house three years before we took over the payments had used this same tank, I had a pretty good idea what had happened.

No sooner than I had my head through the door leading down the steps and into the basement there was the sound of "many waters." The bottom of our late tank had suddenly become a giant shower nozzle and the water was spewing at full force. Already there was a sizeable stream tumbling across the basement floor.

My immediate decision was whether to cut the water off and order a new tank, or leave the water running and stock the new stream with bream, bass and crappie. Realizing that if put to a family vote I would lose by a vote of two to one, I decided for the new tank.

When a tank springs a leak, the only thing to do is to cut the water off until you have a tank that'll hold water. And when a life is so leaky that it is morally unstable, even God must cut off the water of his greatest blessings until the holes in that life can be mended.

Let us not push our analogy too far. But you can no more stop the leaks in an ungodly life with good resolves and high purpose than you can mend a leaking hot-water tank with chewing gum.

When a hot-water tank springs a leak there is no use trying to repair it. The only thing to do is to get a new tank. And the only hope for a person with a leaky, unregenerate heart, is a new heart. And we must get that through repentence and faith in Jesus Christ.

## 48. Certainties Amid the Uncertainties (New Year)

Nothing is so awe inspiring among the experiences which regularly occur as the facing of a new year. At such a time we seem to be face to face with eternity as at no other season. But, actually, the end of one second of time and the beginning of another is equally as significant, for that is the way we live the year round. We are not so conscious of the fact, most of the time, but we are always facing eternity.

David, in flight from jealousy-maddened King Saul, spoke for all of us when he said to Jonathan: ". . . there is but a step between me and death." Who has lived in this world long enough to be a rational creature of even slight maturity without being aware of many close calls with death?

Time and time again the most of us have been miraculously spared when death was but a breath away.

Certainly, one of the things that makes the facing of a new year so awesome is meditation upon the frailties and uncertainties of life and the realization of the grim fact that many you know, perhaps those most dear to you, will depart this life before the year's end. We are constantly "but a step from death."

What, then, are the certainties amid the uncertainties of life? The greatest certainty of all is the fact expressed by Browning:

> Grow old along with me
> The best is yet to be,
> The last of life, for which the first was made.
> Our times are in his hand. . . .

As some one has said, we are immortal till our work on earth is done. But our immortality begins when we are born and this earthly life itself is but a tiny fraction of our immortality, though of tremendous import. For it is in this life we chart our eternal destinies.

All of the other certainties grow out of the beloved fact that our lives are in the hands of God. "If God be for us, who can be against us?" Paul pointed to the great bedrock of the Christian faith as he reminded Timothy that Christ ". . . hath abolished death, and hath brought life and immortality to light through the gospel." Each Christian, with Paul, can face the uncertainties of life with the assurance: ". . . I know whom I have believed, and am persuaded that he is able to keep that which I have committed unto him against that day."

Although we cannot know what the future holds, we know that God holds the future. He has not called us to live the cringing lives of cowards, but, rather, he has called us to walk by faith. "For God hath not given us the spirit of fear; but of power, and of love, and of a sound mind."

Let us step out into the darkness of a new year and place our hand in the hand of God, for as the poet has

said, that will be "better than a light and safer than a known
way."

## 49. Our Greatest Waste (New Year)

"Billy will never have anything — he has never learned
the value of money."

The young man's name we use here is fictitious, but the
young man himself is as real as life. He is well known to
me and to the one who made this statement about him.
And, I fear, his name really is "legion" among the population
of Arkansas and America, for his like among us are many.

Kin to him is the family the head of which said: "I cannot
see that we get along any better with paying our bills now
that the wife works than we did before." For if this family
had learned much about the value of money, they certainly
had not learned the wisdom of living within their income,
which brings them to the same end.

But the failure to recognize the value of money is tied in
with something of even greater significance — the failure
to place the proper value upon one's time. The amount of
money one has may vary from nothing to millions, but each
one of us has the same amount of time — 24 hours every
day we live, no more, no less. The fact that each one of us
is free to use the most of his time as he wishes increases
the weight of our responsibility.

A waste far more to be eschewed than that of wasting
money is that of killing time or using time unwisely. This
is all the more true because we can never know how much
of it we have left. Christ, who had an insight far superior
to any we can have, said: "I must work the works of him
that sent me, while it is day: the night cometh, when no
man can work" (John 9:4).

Dads and mothers in the home cannot afford to waste
hours of parental fellowship and influence, for here they are
giving direction to the destinies of their children. Boys and

girls in schools and colleges cannot afford to waste or misuse precious hours, for school time is the time of building lives and characters for all the future. Even less can we afford to waste the hours of opportunity for worship and walk with God afforded us by our churches.

Our greatest waste is not money or anything else material, but time, for time is life itself.

## 50. "I Went Through Hell . . ." (Easter)

I went through hell itself . . ." said 1st Lt. Thomas G. Smoak, as he told of the harrowing experience he had aboard the B-47 jet plane which mysteriously disintegrated above the city of Little Rock early on the morning of Thursday, March 31, 1960. The plane had taken off just a few minutes before from Little Rock Airforce Base on what had been expected to be an uneventful flight to Houston. But Death was aboard. In just a few minutes more the lives of Smoak's fellow crewmen, along with two Little Rock civilians, were to be snuffed out as the huge plane came apart and plunged in hundreds of flaming pieces into the city below.

The first indication the lone survivor of the plane's crew recalled that all was not well was when he noticed the great ship was listing decidedly to the left. He called the attention of the pilot to this and the pilot righted the plane. But at that instant, Co-Pilot Smoak recalls, "I heard a thud, or a sharp breaking sound, which I didn't know what it was. I have never heard such a noise before. And then everything became very confusing."

The plane was aflame and breaking up, but Smoak could not operate the ejector on the seat in which he was strapped by his safety belt. He tried to release his belt, but his hands were seared by fire. How he escaped he will never know, but a split second later he was free of the plane and floating earthward beneath his parachute.

For one to escape with his life through such an experience

as this is almost as unbelievable as if one should return from the dead. And coming at this Easter season it reminds us of the most remarkable deliverance of all — that of the Lord Jesus Christ from Joseph's new tomb, where he had been dead for three days.

Every one rejoices when a fellow human being has a phenomenal escape from the very jaws of death, as was the experience of Co-Pilot Smoak. But how much greater is the cause for rejoicing as we consider the significance of the victory of Christ over death. For this was a remarkable deliverance for all who will accept it from a fate far worse than physical death. The same power that brought again the Lord Jesus from the dead delivers from eternal death all who will accept Him as Lord and Savior.

But the blessings of Christianity are not mere "pie in the sky, bye and bye," as skeptics would have the world believe. Certainly the Christian can look to the hour of his death and to the Great Beyond with great expectation and un-wavering confidence. The time of our perfection, when we shall be made complete in our Christlikeness, awaits our going to be with the Lord when this earthly life is over. But the blessings of eternal life, of the "more abundant life" which Christ provides through His own death and resurrection are ours from the moment we surrender our hearts to Him.

In this life we are delivered from the penalty of our sins. In this life we are saved from selfishness, from envy, from jealousy, from hatred. In this life we can have the love of God overflowing our hearts. In this life we are able to understand the answers to the great questions of existence: Who am I? Whence did I come? Why am I here? Whither am I headed?

The miraculous power of the risen Lord does what fame, fortune, education, position nor anything else can do — it transforms our natures, it gives us new hearts, it provides for us a true sense of values. Regardless of our outward situations in life, all Christians are ambassadors for Christ, joint-heirs with Him as sons and daughters of the Heavenly Father. Every Christian is a V.I.P. (very important person) in the purpose and providence of God. Every one of us has his post of duty and all of us are immortal until our work here is done.

At this Easter all of us Christians can find peace that passes understanding in verses which had great meaning for Co-Captain Smoak and his wife, both of whom are Christians:

"Therefore we are always confident, knowing that, whilst we are at home in the body, we are absent from the Lord:

"For we walk by faith, not by sight" (II Cor. 5:6-7).

## 51. A Mother's Mark (Mother's Day)

Nancy was too young to help her mother with the dinner to which I had been invited as an honored guest, but she could entertain me as we waited. She showed me the new dress her mother had made for her, she talked with me on many topics, she played the piano for me. But it was at the dinner table she reached the height of her graciousness and thoughtfulness.

On the invitation of Nancy's dad, I "returned thanks." Just as I finished, Nancy beamed a smile of appreciation at me and said, "How nice!"

As the food was being served, Nancy told me it would be all right for me to "take all." At first I thought she meant I might take something from each and every dish. But I soon learned that she was really being generous. If there was something I especially liked I was to take all of it!

It seems that, on a similar occasion, a few days before, when another man had been a dinner guest in the home, the guest had taken the last serving from one of Nancy's own favorite dishes and she was about to protest when her mother had gotten the situation in hand.

As I have thought of this visit with Nancy and with her

two fine brothers older than she, and with her daddy and mother, I have marvelled anew at the wonderful place God has given mothers in shaping the lives of little ones.

She is just four, but already Nancy bears in her character the marks of a marvelous mother, one who not only is teaching her the social graces, but who from the time Nancy was a member of the Cradle Roll has gone with her week after week to church, where she is learning about God and coming to know Him.

I am indebted to *Quests and Conquests,* by Dean C. Dutton, for these thoughts on "Motherhood as a Life Work":

"Just a woman in a Home! Does she need an educational background? What questions of all persons who should have a thousand streams of inspirations it is a Mother in a home.

"Here are monotonies, drudgeries and the thousand little annoyances. If a Mother has streams of thought upspringing from a Paradise carefully builded within — then she can sweep, sew and mend — her hands busy but her head among the stars."

## 52. How Honor the Dead? (Memorial Day)

Today is Memorial Day. What started out to be a day of special remembrance for soldiers who lost their lives in the War Between the States has become a memorial day not only for the dead of all our wars, but for all our dead.

It is fitting that we should have a special day each year to remember our dead and that we should give serious thought to honoring those who lived and died and have gone before us to the Great Beyond. This is a good time for us to ask ourselves a very pointed question: How do you honor the dead?

Cleaning graves, straightening gravestones, and laying beautiful wreaths upon the hallowed mounds is a common practice at this time of the year. And this is as it ought to be. But those of us who are Christian must not have our faith and our hope eclipsed by dark fears of paganism. When we stand at the graves of our loved ones, let us remember the words of the angel at the empty tomb of our Lord: "He is not here, for he is risen."

Certainly we are doing no honor to the departed to imagine they are prisoners of the tombs that hold the dust of their physical bodies. Nor do we honor them when we permit grief to wreck and ruin our own lives and keep us imprisoned in sorrow and despondency for the rest of our earthly days.

How do you honor the dead? How honor the lad who died in the bloom of youth that we Americans might go on being a free people, having freedom from fear, freedom from want, freedom of worship, and freedom of speech?

Not by giving in to fear.

Not by wasting or failing to make proper use of the natural resources handed to us.

Not by living wilful, ungodly lives.

Not by using our freedom of speech to tear down our own government, or keeping quiet and leaving radio, television and the press to those who are selfish and irresponsible.

How honor the dead? How do you honor the memory of a saintly mother, of a God-fearing father? Not merely with grateful tears, as appropriate as they always are, but with purposeful endeavor to be the sons and daughters they longed for us to be: by using our opportunities and heritage to be blessings to others and to help make our nation truly great.

How honor the Saviour, who died for you and rose again and is alive forever more? Not by cowering at the thought of physical death, but by the sure-footed walk of faith that proclaims to all the world and to the heavens:

"Because he lives, we shall live also."

"Brethren, I count not myself to have apprehended: but this one thing I do, forgetting those things which are behind, and reaching forth unto those things which are before,

"I press toward the mark for the prize of the high calling of God in Christ Jesus."

We honor the memory of our loved ones with nothing

we can buy. We honor them, if we honor them at all, with the lives we live.

We honor our Christ, who died and is now alive forever — if we honor him at all — with consecrated hearts and dedicated heads, hands, and feet.


## 53. Our Greatest Treasure (Children's Day)

In the year 1284, legend has it, the town of Hamelin, Germany, was overrun by rats. The town fathers did everything they could to be rid of the vermin, but to no avail.

Deliverance came from an unexpected source. A strange fellow forever afterwards to be known as The Pied Piper of Hamelin appeared on the scene and declared he could get rid of the rats.

That was while the town was still under the curse, and the councilmen were all ears and open purses. They agreed to pay a tidy sum for the piper's remedy. So he took out his fife and began to walk through the streets toward the River Weser, piping a strange and monotonous tone. Immediately rats began appearing from everywhere. They kept coming until they were all following the Pied Piper in a tumultuous torrent.

With an eye for collecting his fee, the Piper led them into the river and all were drowned.

But when he went to collect, the aldermen had decided that now the rats were gone they would not pay the amount they had agreed upon.

The sad conclusion was that the Piper again marched through the streets and again he piped a strange note. This time all the children of the town went scurrying out to follow him. He led them out of the town to a mountain which opened and received them. The mountain closed behind them, so the story ends, and no one ever saw them again. We do not have space to draw any lengthy conclusions.

All will agree that our greatest treasure is our boys and girls and that there are many evil influences trying to lead them astray. One of the greatest safeguards for our children is our own love and understanding. We found this the other day in *Quests and Conquests,* by Dean Dutton:

"I shall make it my business to love and notice children. I shall know large numbers of them by name. In my absence I shall write them post cards with a 'God bless you.'

"I shall take it as one of my sweetest, richest, fullest ministries to be a real friend to little children.

"Sacred to the future of my country, sacred to the hearth-stone of American nobility; sacred to a pure faith, noble character, and lofty aims and ideals, it shall be my high resolve to cultivate a helpful friendship with these angels of the morning of life."

## 54. Trusting in Father (Father's Day)

We are indebted to Dean C. Dutton for the story about some botanists, a rare flower and an Alpine shepherd boy.

A group of naturalists who were searching in the Alps for rare specimens of flowers discovered a beautiful flower on a rock ledge they could not reach. Calling to a nearby shepherd boy, they offered him several shining coins if he would allow himself to be let down by them by a rope to secure the flower.

The boy very much wanted to earn the money. He looked at the men, all strangers, and he looked at the precipice between them and the flower and he declined.

Again they persuaded him and he was almost ready to accept their offer. He looked into the precipice, he looked at the money, but then he looked into the faces of the strangers and again the answer was a negative shake of his head.

Then a bright idea came to him. "Wait here till I come back," he said, and he darted away to a mountain cabin.

Soon the lad returned with a giant mountaineer. "I will get the flower for you," he said, "if you will let my father help hold the rope."

And now we quote Dr. Dutton:

"Yes, yes, down into the valley of sorrow if that must be, down into the gorge of pain; we can safely go anywhere if our loving heavenly Father holds the rope.

"Prayer is the life line in God's blessed hands. How carefully he holds us in the darkest and most uncertain hours. But, how safe we are.

" 'He knoweth our frame. He remembereth that we are dust.'

" 'I will never leave thee nor forsake thee.'

" 'Fear thou not for I am with thee; be not dismayed. I am they God. I will strengthen thee; yea, I will help thee; yea, I will uphold thee with the right hand of my righteousness.'

"He was near with Abraham on his mountain with Isaac.

"He was with Moses at the Red Sea.

"Everything came out just right with Jacob, Joseph and Benjamin.

"He was with Daniel in the den of lions; with the three Hebrew children. He refreshed Elijah by the coming of the angel. He never fails. He always has His own big, BIG plans. . . ."

And yet so many of us insist on going our own floundering ways!

## 55. Uniform Lovers (Fourth of July)

A civilian who likes to wear military uniforms but who, apparently, does not care for the responsibilities and hardship of military service, broke into trouble and the news again here recently.

According to press reports, it was the eighth time in five years for twenty-one-year-old John Dominic Pinnelli, of Dallas,

Tex., to be sentenced for illegally wearing an Army, Navy or Air Force uniform.

In each of the first six instances, the young man is reported to have received a six-month sentence, and, on the seventh occasion, a probationary sentence for one year.

Following the September sentence Pinnelli, it is reported, was given transportation from Little Rock to Dallas where he was to have stayed on a job as directed by the terms of his sentence. But about a month later, on October 27, he was arrested in Albuquerque, N. M., again for illegally wearing a uniform!

In a hearing in Little Rock before Judge J. Smith Henley, in federal district court, Pinnelli's probation was revoked and he was sentenced under the Youth Corrections Act, which means that the U. S. Board of Parole will release him when the board feels he is ready for release — any time up to four years.

Said the judge in pronouncing the latest sentence: "If I could, I would give you a license to wear a uniform. But I can't and it's against the law to wear one unless you're in military service."

How many of us are seekers for places of honor and esteem but who have no desire or intention of shouldering the responsibility that goes with the positions? Is not this about the same situation? We like the uniform of distinction but we are not ready to distinguish ourselves through sacrificial service.

The ordinance of baptism, the door to church membership constitutes itself something of a uniform which the new Christian puts on before all the world, declaring himself to be a soldier of Christ. But how many put on this uniform to their shame, refusing to take up the cross that goes with it?

No court in the land has jurisdiction over cases of false wearers of the uniform of the Christian profession. But there is a higher Court with which we all must reckon.

## 56. Christmas Recollections (Christmas)

My earliest recollections of Christmas are pretty well
dominated by the material. It makes me blush to confess
it, but there were a few Christmases back in my early days
when my main concern was what was olde Santa going
to bring me, olde Erv.

Either we kids of my generation were dumber than kids
today, or Santa is dumber today than he was when us old
heads wre growing up. We actually believed, and there was
some convincing evidence that it was so, that there was
a real connection between our conduct and Santa's liberality.
Although it never happened to me, there was always the
very real possibility that Santa would bring a boy who had
been mean, a bundle of switches for Christmas. (This was
a "present" some of us found to our stinging discomfort
was not restricted to the holiday season.)

Now I can't remember too many Christmases by dates.
Rather, I remember them by what I got. There was the
drum-and-bugle Christmas. That was one of the first I can
remember. And I dare say that this one was long remembered
by all who were close enough to be entertained by me as
I performed.

Not long after that, a year or maybe two, was my monkey-
climbing-a-string Christmas. Then there were in succession
my little-red-wagon Christmas, my chopping axe and handsaw
Christmas (I deadened half the trees on Bunker Hill before
my parents caught me and explained that if I chopped the
bark off all the way around a tree the tree would die.)

One of my biggest Christmases was my farm-wagon Christmas. That was the year Uncle Robert got me that big farm
wagon I had wished for all year out of the big Sears, Roebuck
catalog.

Another fine Christmas was my .22-rifle Christmas. I sure
made the bird feathers fly with that. The pop of a gun
sure shoos the birds!

Along with the Christmas tree program each year at the

London Baptist Church, there was always a Christmas program. All of us kids had parts, singing, giving dialogs, acrostics, or "saying speeches." This was largely a "necessary evil" for us kids — somthing we had to do and get out of the way before the presents would be given out from the Christmas tree and old Santa would come through — scaring the babies and giving cheap candy to everybody.

But as the years have passed, some of the parts I had on the Christmas programs have come surging back through my consciousness and sub-consciousness, to take their places along with the remembrance of the smell of cedar, burned fire-cracker powder, exploded "torpedoes," fresh-peeled oranges, etc. Some of the songs we sang and the scriptures we quoted have come to have real meaning across the years.

It's easy now to see that the famous Bethlehem inn is not the only place that had no room for the Lord. Our crowded hearts have been too full of "Christmas" time after time for the Lord Himself to come in. Will this be the year the Lord will have first place in our hearts and homes at Christmas?


## 57. What for Christmas? (Christmas)

"What do you want for Christmas?" "What's Olde Santa going to bring you?"

These are questions we have heard all our lives at this time of the year, and we are still hearing them.

Well, what *do* you want for Christmas?

Some things that used to be common and acceptable as Christmas presents are no longer to be had or desired, except as antiques. We are thinking of the cups with the moustache guards that Mamma used to give Papa. Also, there was the coal oil lamp with its beautifully flowered shade that Papa and the kiddies used to give Mamma — a present no less acceptable because it was something the whole family could use and enjoy.

Time and space fail us to mention such things as andirons ("dogirons"), coffee grinders, single or double-bit axes, cross-cut saws, sausage-grinders and dozens of other things which may or may not still be on the market but which, because of our present way of life, are not considered essential to the efficient operation of a modern home.

"But," some will be asking, "what did these things ever have to do with what people wanted for Christmas?"

Well, kind friends, before we all got to living like kings and queens, flitting around in cars or lolling on couches or sprawling in easy chairs to watch television, the most of us had to work for a living. And we had to live on a lot less than what we call necessities today.

It used to be that people had to be far more practical in their Christmas shopping than now. Aside from a few toys, like dolls, popguns, and monkeys-on-strings, what we bought for Christmas presents had to have a year-round utility.

What do you want for Christmas?

A happy Christmas is not assured merely by what can be tied in tinsel and ribbon. It is to be found only in the hearts of men and women and boys and girls who, through the greatest gift of all, the Lord Jesus Christ, have been transformed into people of goodwill, eternally in love with God and with the people of all ranks and nations. Where the love of Christ abides there will be happiness at Christmas and throughout the future, whether the possessor be young or old, wealthy or poor, healthy or ill, and regardless of the station in life or color of skin. Christ has given us His peace. And he has overcome the world.

Regardless of what you may give or receive at Christmas, may you have Christ, the gift of our loving Heavenly Father to a lost world.

## 58. Paying the Toll

Going to mill used to be a weekly or every-other-week affair, down on Bunker. That was back when Poor Richard's admonition about plowing deep while sluggards sleep seemed awfully personal.

Getting ready to go to mill was something that required the services of "all hands and the cook." Dad and Mother and the kids that were big enough to be of any help would take a big dishpan and a meal sack and go to the corn crib. There we would select choice ears of corn and proceed to "shuck" the corn and then shell it into the dishpan.

We did not have a corn shelling machine. They had been invented, but you still had to pay for them. We just used our hands, or, if the friction was too great for the palms, corncobs could be used to press the grains of corn off the cob.

When we had the dishpan full, we'd pour the corn into the meal sack, tie the top of the sack with a piece of fishing cord, and soon be off for London and George Martin's grist mill.

Sometimes the round trip of six miles would be made by muleback. Then you would mount the mule and throw the bag of corn across the mule, in front of you, so that the corn would be about half on one side and half on the other and you would have no difficulty holding it in place. But the most of the time we made the trip in the farm wagon.

For a long time I thought Miller George Martin was one of the most accommodating fellows I had ever seen. That was before I learned that you don't get something for nothing. But one day I discovered that he was not running the mill just out of the goodness of his heart and for the accommodation of his friends and neighbors. I caught him taking a big hand scoop of a thing and dipping it full of *our* corn and pouring it over into *his* own bin! I was about to call the constable when my Dad explained that the miller was supposed to have his toll.

Since then I have been pretty conscious of the toll. The

toll is not always as evident as it was at Mr. Martin's mill, nor as just, but it is always there. Much of the toll we pay in life is just and necessary. But a lot of toll is exorbitant and that which we can ill afford to pay. Look out for the toll.

A lot of people are having their corn ground at the devil's mill. And the devil does not take his toll out of the corn, he takes it out of your manhood or womanhood. Regardless of what the meal is you are having ground, this is a toll you cannot afford.


## 59. "Is This My Room?"

For this boy from Bunker Hill — that's about two miles from Mill Creek and not far from The Flatwoods — Miami Beach, Forida, is about as fabulous and swanky as any place he has read about in *Arabian Nights*. But that was not his first impression on checking in at a Miami Beach hotel the other day.

It was late afternoon as a bellboy helped me to my room. The room was in semi-darkness but the guide did not turn on the lights as we entered. I was a little puzzled. But he seemed to know his way around as he hung my other shirt in the walk-in closet and checked to see that everything in the room was up to his requirements.

By this time my eyes had become somewhat accustomed to the darkness and I had been able to determine that the room was commodious and that it had all of the usual furnishings you find in a twin-bed room you rent at the single rate. But in my mind I was grumbling.

"Huh!" I was thinking. "What's so wonderful about a room here? I have been in fairly swank hotels before. What does this one have that is different from dozens of inland hotels where I have slept across the country? I thought Miami Beach was to be something special!"

The bellboy had completed his services for me, I thought,

and I gave him his tip. But instead of walking toward the door, he turned to the back side of the room, which was covered from one end to the other by drapes.

Dramatically he rolled back the curtains and there was the Atlantic Ocean! I almost swallowed my tongue. Standing in my own room — one I had thought was just another hotel room and a dark one at that — I was looking out upon "the ocean." There it was, lapping and moaning beneath my window, and stretching out as far as the eye could see. with many a boat in between! I had judged my room too soon!

You, too, if you have lived very long, have at times asked in your heart as you have stood in the darkness of sorrow, of disappointment, of affliction, of temptation: "Is this my room?" Then God has rolled back curtains revealing marvelous picture windows you had not known were there. Suddenly you have found yourself looking out upon an ocean of His love and providence!

## 60. Johnson Grass

It's hard for those of us who have spent a big part of our lives fighting grass — in the cotton and corn patches and in our yards — to realize that the grasses "are first among all families of the plant kingdom in their usefulness to man."

There are 4,700 different kinds of grasses, but just one Johnson grass.

At one stretch along the roadside between my house and the office is a luxuriant patch of Johnson grass. (Ever see any Johnson grass that was not luxuriant?)

A few weeks ago I saw a workman spraying the Johnson grass with some kind of chemical. I thought about stopping to tell him he could get rid of Johnson grass in but one way — digging it up. But it was none of my never-mind.

A day or two later, all the grass was as dead as a door

knob. Or so it appeared. Although the temperature was ranging in the upper eighties, the late grass had the appearance of having been snowed under by a quarter-inch frost.

Maybe I had been wrong. Maybe you could get rid of Johnson grass just by pouring something on it. Wish we'd had some of that spray down on Bunker when I was growing up. It would have added several years to my life expectancy!

For several days I was out of town and I forgot about the Johnson grass. Then I suddenly found myself driving along that desolate strip again. Desolate? Like a fish! There was a whole new crop of Johnson pushing right up through the dead grass tops and about half as high already as it was the day the patch had been sprayed.

Our bent to sinning, sometimes called "the Adamic nature," is a lot like Johnson grass. It can be sprayed with good intentions, with reformation, with "clean, ethical living," and for a while it will seem to have died. But the roots of degeneration are still there, sprouting a whole new crop.

The only relief from our sinful natures is through a death and a birth — the death of the old man of sin and the birth through regeneration of the new man as a true son of God. Nothing we can rub on the outsides of our lives will bring this about. It comes only through the miraculous power of Jesus Christ, by grace through faith.


## 61. Our Only Refuge

Geography never was one of my favorite subjects in school. I always got lost in the maze of facts about so many places that were so far away from Bunker Hill. But there were a lot of interesting pictures to look at in those big geography books that were in use 40 years ago.

One of the most fascinating things to us children who used to have to help mend the fences to keep the cows out of the corn were pictures of the Great Wall of China —

a wall 25 feet wide at the base, 25 feet high and 1,500 miles long!

What a wall! And they say it was started about 200 years before the birth of Christ.

It seems that from the earliest times men have had cause to be afraid of fellow men. The China Wall was built to keep out the enemy tribes of Northern Asia. All the way across it, every 200 to 300 yards, is a watchman's tower. For hundreds of years, the wall withstood assault after assault from the enemy.

Then, we are told, one day a man who had the innocent appearance of a simple shepherd approached the wall and engaged one of the guards in conversation. The guard had been drinking intoxicants and his own wall was down. Soon the "shepherd" was successful in bribing him to open a gate just for a few minutes.

No sooner was the gate open than hordes of marauders from everywhere were swarming in. The wall that had been a wall of defense for a thousand years did not fall — it is still standing. But one watchman failed. And the wall was no stronger than its weakest watchman.

As recent as World War II, a nation of people, the French, were counting on a great defense line, the Maginot Line, to keep the enemy out. But Hitler's Panzer units scarcely slowed down, in driving across the Maginot Line to take France.

Today we are more concerned than ever about an adequate defense. The oceans that used to serve as protective barriers are now open highways to enemy submarines. Our cities are in the sights of Russian missile-launching devices. There literally are no places to hide.

God is the world's only refuge:

"Except the Lord build the house, they labor in vain that build it: except the Lord keep the city, the watchman waketh but in vain" (Ps. 127:1).

## 62. Consulting the Purse

"Ere fancy you consult, consult your purse," declared
Benjamin Franklin's Poor Richard.

This reminds me of an embarrasing moment for Papa and
me one time when I consulted my fancy (appetite) without
first consulting his purse.

As an eight-year-old boy I had been given the high privilege
of going with Papa in our farm wagon "to town" — Russellville, the county seat of Pope County. The fact that I had
no money was of no great concern to me. I was used to
it. Getting to make the sixteen-mile round trip from "down
on Bunker," where we lived, and seeing the sights of "the
big city" was treat enough. Russellville must have had more
than four thousand residents by that time.

Everything went well till we were about ready to start
back home. Before driving our mules out to the big, concrete,
circular watering place that stood at that time at the end
of Russellville's Main Street, Papa took me into a drug store
that had what they called a "soda fountain." (The only
kind of soda I had heard of up till then was baking soda.)

"Give us two cokes," Papa said, as he and I stood in front
of the fountain and looked at ourselves in the big looking
glass back of it.

But I had already seen a rough sketch of a big milkshake
on the edge of the mirror. I had never had a milkshake.
In fact, till then I had not known that such a thing existed
"on God's green earth," as old Doc, the traveling veterinarian,
used to say. But I decided I must have one.

Made bold by my new desire, I spoke out as unrestrainedly
as if I had been in my usual and familiar surroundings,
back on Bunker. "I wanna milkshake," I said.

"Huh-uh, Son, take a coke," said Papa.

"No, I wanna milkshake," I insisted, before I noticed the
troubled look on Papa's face.

"Give him a coke," Papa told the man, and that settled it.
When we had finished our nickel drinks — I believe

they called them "fountain cokes" — and we were outside and headed for the wagon yard, Papa said: "Son, you must be careful what you ask for when we are out like that. Milkshakes cost 15 cents and Papa didn't have the money to get you one."

The milkshake has long been one of my favorites, but I never drink one without a pang of remorse as I remember the way I embarrassed Papa. He wanted me to have that milkshake, but it was not in his power to give it to me.

How different with our Heavenly Father. He has unlimited resources "according to his riches in glory by Christ Jesus."

## 63. A Glimpse of Eternity

One day recently, in the twinkling of an eye, I had a glimpse of eternity. It was a cold day. A friend and I were driving across town. I was the driver and the most of my attention was necessarily focused on the street and the traffic. But at one point along the way I saw two men unloading a stretcher from the rear of an ambulance. In the split second as we passed I could see that the stretcher bore a form wrapped head and foot.

"Someone has died," I said to my friend.

My friend made no reply. Soon there were other things to claim our attention.

Who had died? What had been the status of this one in life? Had he lived in a spacious and beautiful residence in an exclusive section, or had he lived in a hovel? Did he have a good income, with much property, or was he penniless? Did he travel first class, or was he a hitchhiker? It mattered not. He had gone out of life as he had come — empty-handed. Whatever property he had owned would now change hands.

Had this person been popular? Had he many friends? Or was he a castaway, scorned and shunned? Either way, he had travelled alone when his time had come.

Was he a loving husband, a father who basked in the love of sons and daughters? A good neighbor, a law-abiding citizen? Or was he a hermit who shunned the normal relationships of life? Either way he had died.

But here is the most searching question of all. Was he saved or lost? Did he know Jesus Christ as Lord and Saviour? While he was living could he say with Paul ". . . I know whom I have believed and am persuaded that he is able to keep that which I have committed unto him against that day"? If so, he had not really died. If not, he had already entered into eternal death.

In one split second I had had a glimpse of eternity. The one whose lifeless form was being carried into the funeral parlors was Everyman.

But this is not the end of the story. Jesus died and rose again. And because He lives we shall live also!

In this glimpse of eternity everything else fades into insignificance in the face of this searching question: Saved or lost?

## 64. In His Own Image

A striking monument to self is one of the feature attractions in the Ripley "Belive It or Not" Odditorium in New York City.

As you enter the museum, you are immediately attracted to a life-like statue in wood of a rather diminutive middle-aged oriental man dressed only in a loincloth. Over the exhibit, which continually revolves at moderate speed, are the words: "Man or Image?"

You read that this likeness is a self portrait sculptured by an artist, supposedly in true proportion and full life size, and that the artist used for the statue his own hair and his own fingernails and toenails.

Obviously, here was a man who dreaded, perhaps above everything else, the oblivion of physical death. He did not want his image to disappear from the walks of men. Or he may have believed, as did many of the ancients, that his life after death depended upon the continuing existence of a body for his soul to inhabit.

At any rate, he has achieved for himself a sort of earthly immortality. Of course, his wooden image, with its real hair, real fingernails and toenails, and with its sparkling, life-like eyes behind his own spectacles, will some day become dust or ashes.

Job spoke for Everyman when he asked, thousands of years ago, "If a man die, shall he live again?"

The answer seemed, on outward appearances, to be no: "There is hope of a tree, if it be cut down, that it will sprout again, and that the tender branch thereof will not cease," reasoned Job. ". . . But man dieth, and wasteth away: yea, man giveth up the ghost, and where is he?

"As the waters fail from the sea, and the flood decayeth and drieth up:

"So man lieth down, and riseth not. . . ."

But God answered the hungering in Job's heart and Job was eventually able to respond with one of the great affirmations of God's revelation to man:

". . . I know that my redeemer liveth, and that he shall stand at the latter day upon the earth:

"And though after my skin worms destroy this body, yet in my flesh shall I see God. . . ."

For Christians, trusting in Christ who gives us the victory over death, we ". . . know that, when he shall appear, we shall be like him; for we shall see him as he is" (I John 3:2b).

## 65. Freedom from Fear

On January 6, 1941, President Franklin D. Roosevelt, eleven months before Japan's Pearl Harbor attack, delivered his famous "four freedoms" address to Congress. As a basis for world peace, the President proposed for all people: freedom of speech, freedom of worship, freedom from want and freedom from fear.

To a large extent man can himself provide the first three freedoms. But only God can give us freedom from fear.

The Psalmist, in Psalm 23, reveals the secret of this freedom:

*Yea, though I walk through the valley of the shadow of death, I will fear no evil: for thou art with me; thy rod and thy staff they comfort me.*

"*. . . for thou art with me. . . .*"

Ellis A. Fuller used to tell about an experience involving him and his son, Ellis, Jr. The surgeon had said that Ellis, Jr., then a little boy, must have his tonsils removed. "I will have my tonsils out if you will go with me to the operating room and then stay with me the rest of the day," Ellis, Jr., bargained.

Dr. Fuller, then pastor of First Baptist Church, Atlanta, and a member of the Georgia Baptist Hospital board, agreed. "Pulling his brass," he got himself admitted to the operating room for the operation and then went with his son to his hospital room to stay with him through the day.

That was before the days of air-conditioning, and Dr. Fuller recalled that the heat was oppressive and his son's suffering rather acute. Toward the end of the day the little boy took his daddy's hand and said: "Dad, it was worth it just to have you with me all day."

What a wonderful thought for Christians that our Heavenly Father is always with us in our afflictions, ". . . our refuge and strength, a very present help in trouble. . . ."

We need fear no evil, for God is present with us as the Good Shepherd who loves his sheep and gives himself for them. He is not like the hirelings, who run away when the wolves come and leave the sheep to their fate.

God is with us as the Good Shepherd who provides for all our needs — ". . . I shall not want. He maketh me to lie down in green pastures: he leadeth me beside the still water. . . ."

God is with us as the Good Shepherd who will see us through the dark shadows and will guide us safely home. We will fear no evil!

## 66. Greatest Stoop

"Greatest Stoop in the World," is the title of an interesting feature in the January 15, 1959 issue of R. G. LeTourneau's little magazine, *Now*.

Here Stuart P. Garver tells about a mayor of the city of Boston, Massachusetts, and an experiment the mayor carried out, many years ago, in an effort to "find out how the other half of the world lives."

After he had a several days' growth of beard, the mayor dressed himself in the apparel of a tramp and went into the slum sections of Boston. At the close of the day he applied at a cheap boarding house for over-night lodging. He was told he would be provided bed and breakfast upon his promise to chop a quantity of firewood the next morning.

Now the mayor had never tried before to wield an axe. When he got around to his wood-cutting chore, he found the going even harder than he had imagined it would be. But in the midst of his predicament, a young man stepped to his side. "Let me have the axe," he said, "for I can see that you know nothing about chopping wood."

Soon the young man had completed the task. The disguised mayor took from an inside pocket one of his cards. Handing it to the young man, he said: "Report to me at my office this afternoon at 4 o'clock and I will see that you are given a good job."

The young man took the card, but he thought to himself: "Poor fellow. He's crazy. He thinks he is the Mayor."

But the youth's curiosity got the better of him during the day and 4 p.m. found him at the mayor's office. He was ushered into the presence of the man he had thought was a crazy hobo, but he now found him shaven and dressed as becoming one of the high office he held.

As he had promised, the mayor assigned the young man to a good-paying position. But he made one specific request: The young man was to tell no one about the mayor's slumming experience.

But like the man Jesus healed with the admonition to keep the healing secret, this young fellow went out and told the thrilling story. Someone on the staff of a Boston daily newspaper heard it and the paper carried the mayor's story under the big headline: "The Greatest Social Stoop in the World."

But this "stoop," as Mr. Garver points out, "is pallid, insipid, when compared with the stoop our blessed Lord accomplished when He humbled Himself to become our Savior. His, indeed, is the greatest stoop in all the world (Phil. 2:8)."

## 67. Self Gets in the Way

Several years ago, while serving as director of public relations of the Southern Baptist Seminary in Louisville, I had frequent contact with the members of the staffs of Louisville's two great dailies — *The Courier-Journal* and *The Louisville Times*. One day I had taken a distinguished visitor to the newspaper offices to be interviewed. As a photographer was setting up to make a portrait shot, I said to the visitor in the cameraman's presence: "You are about to have your picture made by one of the best news photographers in the country."

The photographer, a personal friend of mine and one who deserved the compliment, was noticeably embarrassed. He smiled an acknowledgement through his blushes, fired the usual two camera shots, and released us.

As we were walking out to the news offices, the photographer came running after us. "Come back," he said in greater embarrassment than before, "I forgot to pull the slides!"

By causing my friend to shift his center of interest from his photographic subject and from his camera and lights to himself, I had caused him to fail. In his frustration he had done everything he usually does in making a picture but one vital step. The tripping of his camera shutter and the flashing of lights synchronized with the shutter had been to no avail. He had not removed the slides from his film holders, and so the film had not been exposed. If he had developed the film he would have had blanks.

The radiance of a Christian's life shines bright because of the miracle of the new birth. So long as one's thoughts and concern center on one's own self, one's own business, one's own family, one's own things, one's life will be a blank. Not until faith in Jesus Christ leads to the pulling of the slides of self-centeredness can the light of God's redeeming love get through to work its miracle on the magic film of the human soul.

It is significant that Jesus mentions self-denial first, in stating what it means to be his disciple: "If any man will come after me, let him deny himself, take up his cross, and follow me" (Matt. 16:24).


## 68. Heaven from a Housetop

Housetops used to serve more useful purposes than merely to keep out the elements, down on Bunker Hill. During the late summer and early fall, we used to cut up peaches and apples and spread them out on the housetop to dry. Getting the fruit off the ground level and into the direct rays of the sun not only assured the quickest and surest curing process, but it tended to keep away contaminating swarms of hungry flies.

There was another use of the housetop that appealed to me as a boy. That was cloud gazing. With no television or radio, with few books and magazines, and with not many places to go or sights to see, you could climb the leaning ladder to the shingle-roof top of the house and amuse yourself by the hour, watching the clouds fly over on a lazy summer's day.

Of course, the clouds could be watched from the ground. But you seemed to have a more direct contact from the housetop.

"Pearly White City" was a song that was being heard a lot in those days. This, along with the influence of a large, illustrated family Bible, helped me to visualize "the New Jerusalem" in some of the colorful clouds.

Something one of the speakers at a recent evangelistic conference said brought my long-ago, housetop experience back afresh. He said that Christians are no longer living in daily expectation of the coming again of the Lord Jesus Christ.

We have developed varying attitudes about the second coming of Christ. Some, the plain teachings of the Scriptures to the contrary notwithstanding, claim they can tell you the day and the hour this great event is to occur. But the most of us, it seems, are just not thinking much about it, if at all.

Is it not something greatly to be deplored if we find in searching our hearts that heaven and the coming again of the Lord seemed much more imminent when we were children than now that we are mature men and women?

What greater encouragement can Christians have to help them "stand in the evil day" of this present generation than the knowledge of the fact that Christ is most assuredly coming again, and that he may come today?

". . . why stand ye gazing up into heaven? this same Jesus, which is taken up from you into heaven, shall so come in like manner . . ." (Acts 1:11).

## 69. The Silent Cuckoo

Several years ago a relative gave our family a cuckoo clock — one of those works of art-in-wood made in the Black Forest area of Germany. We assembled it, placed it in a prominent position in our living room, and began enjoying the novelty of the little "cuckoo" that would poke its head out on the hour to call "cuckoo" for each count.

But it was not long until the cockoo went on a strike — it stopped striking the hour. The faithful hands of the clock would move around and around the face of the clock but the cuckoo's door would never open.

We could have taken the clock to a shop and had it repaired. But it was keeping good time and we just let it run sans-cuckoo.

After the silence of the cuckoo had run into weeks, months, and years, one of our nephews who is mechanically inclined was visiting us one day and he discovered that the cuckoo part of our clock was not "cukooing." "Why don't you fix it?" he asked. "There really is nothing wrong with the cuckoo — its chain is off the sprocket."

Grabbing a pair of plyers and a strand of wire, he went to work and soon had the long silent cuckoo back on duty. The clock that had been made to be a cuckoo clock was again more than just a clock.

The great loss in the world today is not the countless millions of tons of water that go over the falls unharnessed, nor the wide expanses of land left fallow, nor anything else in the physical universe. Rather it is the lack of abundance in the living we do from day to day as we settle for just living or existing.

Life was never meant to be humdrum or cheap. That was not a part of God's design when he made us to be in his image. The Greek word for "man" — "*anthropos*" — meaning "the looking-up one," sets us apart in God's creation as His masterpiece.

Potentially, every one of us has life in the fullest sense

of the word. Many changes can come and much can go wrong
in our environments, but, as the cuckoo clock with its chain
in place on the sprocket wheel is the novelty it was designed
to be, we can still be the persons God made us to be. It
is when something goes wrong inside of us — when the chain
of our faith in Christ that runs from our little hearts to the
great heart of God gets off-track — that we drop from
abundant living to just living.

## 70. Sputnik

You never know what new word the next edition of the
daily paper will bring you these days.

One of the thrills of living is hearing and learning new
words. I can remember the first time I ever heard the
word "program." I should for I was past six and a first-grader
at Lone Gum. I ran most of the three miles home that
day to tell my folks that teacher had "put me on the program."
But, en route, I got my philology mixed up with a history
lesson, and what I actually announced to my puzzled parents
was: "Teacher has put me on the Pilgrim."

Until recently, if we had heard someone muttering
the word "sputnik" we would have thought he had laryngitis
or that he had missed an appointment with his psychiatrist.
But now everybody knows about sputnik, the Russian word
for the first man-made satellite to be launched successfully
into outer space. And the object for which the new word
stands is travelling around the earth in its orbit between 500
and 600 miles above the earth and at a speed of 18,000
miles an hour. Broken down, this means sputnik scoots five
miles while you are saying "Jack Robinson."

Sputnik will have its place in the history books and the
dictionaries from now on, for, almost surely, it marks the
beginning of a new scientific age. Not even the scientists
will attempt at this time to predict what the Russian moon

portends for the world and mankind in the future, or even in the next few years.

Will man turn the new gadgets into lethal weapons to destroy in the twinkling of an eye whole countries or even continents? Or will man make use of his new scientific achievements to expand and broaden opportunities for living? Will we soon be going to the moon on week-end excursions, or, possibly, to some of the planets?

Some are suggesting that, in the event of atomic warfare on earth, some of the human race may escape to the moon. But, unless there is a big change in the quality of our lives, we'd soon be having war on the moon. It appears we may be able to move to the moon before we have learned how to live on the earth!

While there are many questions about sputnik and the sputnik era that cannot yet be answered, certainly not by this columnist, there are some things relating to it that can be known as of now. The world without Christ still is lost. Science can never provide the way of escape from our sins. Christ is still the hope of the world.

## 71. Back to Big Culvert

Several months ago now I shared with the readers of this column an experience I had of going back to what had been a wonderful swimming and fishing hole in my boyhood — Big Culvert, on the Missouri Pacific Railroad a mile or two west of London — only to find the hole was dried up.

What a shock this was on the hot summer day of my eager trek, loaded with fishing tackle and a can of red-worms. What a tremendous disappointment. Perhaps it was in an effort to salvage something worthwhile from the experience that this columnist turned philosophic and answered:

"There are many 'Big Culverts' along life's way. Many a life that showed great promise in its youth has dried up. Some who made the honor rolls in school and college have turned out to be miserable failures in the hard school of life itself. . . ."

Well, the other day I was paying a visit to an old friend at London, George Dawson, who lives pretty close to Big Culvert, and he was telling me about a nice mess of big bream he had caught just recently. And where do you suppose he caught them? Yes, you are right. He caught them out of Big Culvert!

The hole that I had written off my books as being eternally dry and desolate again has water and fish in it! Just a moment, please, while I put my philosophy cap back on!

It seems to me that this latest happening at Big Culvert has an even more inspiring lesson for us than the earlier. Are there not many lives that have been marked off the books of some of us as worthless that, given the right encouragement at the right time, flourish again?

It used to be that people who had lived from forty to fifty years were "old folks," and there was a saying, "You can't teach an old dog new tricks." But somebody finally found out that older people could go on expanding in interests and usefulness. No wonder the book, *Life begins at Forty,* turned out to be a best seller.

Certainly it is true in the spiritual, above all other facets of life, that life can begin at any time. The fact that one's life has been a failure up to now is no reason why it must go on being a failure.

As Ezekiel's experience in the valley of dry bones, the skeletons of lives which have long borne the mark of spiritual desolation and death, through the regenerating power of the Lord Jesus Christ can be made to live again. The refreshed Big Culvert stands as a symbol of hope for all whose lives have dried up.

## 72. "God Is Good to Us"

A few Sundays ago I was the supply preacher for a church

in north central Arkansas and met again, for the first time in many years, a man and his wife who had been fellow church members and dear friends of mine a long time ago.

They invited me to their home for lunch and we had opportunity to review the swift years since we had last been together.

"The Lord has been good to me," said the husband, who is now three score years and ten. "And he has been good to my wife," he added, quickly.

"Now I agree with you that the Lord has been good to you," I quipped. "But when you say He has been good to your wife — well, I don't know about that!"

He got the point and we had a laugh together.

"The Lord has been good to me." How often we say this or hear it said. But how childish we often are in judging or evaluating God's goodness.

Many a Christian thinks there is good only in the things that give pleasure or delight. Business is good — our health is good — "The Lord is good!" But it is not so easy for us to see that God is no less good to us in sickness, in adversity, in poverty, in sorrow.

Paul took a wide view of the experiences of life. He had learned as a Christian fully yielded to the Lord that God never ceases to be good to His children.

The difference for Christians is not that suffering and sorrow never come, but that ". . . all things work together for good to them that love God. . . ."

Like the tree planted by the rivers of water, the Christian grows and prospers and fulfills God's purpose for his life, through the rains of life as well as the sunshine.

The trials that come to us serve to keep us from anchoring our lives to the things of this world, which are always passing away, and turn us anew into the haven of rest found only in Christ.

Romans 8:28 is a light for Christians they can count on in their darkest nights.

## 73. Closer Than a Brother

According to Aesop, as quoted in a school reader of a few generations ago:

Two fellows were travelling together through a wood when a bear rushed out upon them. One of the travelers happened to be in front, and he seized hold of the branch of a tree and hid himself among the leaves.

The other, seeing no help for it, threw himself flat down upon the ground, with his face in the dust.

The bear, coming up to him, put his muzzle close to his ear, and sniffed and sniffed. But at last with a growl he shook his head and slouched off, for bears will not touch dead meat.

Then the fellow in the tree came down to his comrade and, laughing, said, "What was it that Master Bruin whispered to you?"

"He told me," said the other, " 'Never trust a friend who deserts you in a pinch.' "

The prodigal son of the parable in Luke 15 learned "the hard way" that many who pose as your friends during the properous times when you are playing host will desert you in the pinch of poverty and want.

Joseph experienced the inhumanity of man to man in the heartless actions of his own brothers who first abandoned him in a pit and later sold him into slavery.

Perhaps few who have lived any length of time have been spared the rude awakening that comes with finding out that some who have been trusted as loved ones and friends have withheld or withdrawn their affection and good will.

But Christ is a friend who "sticketh closer than a brother," one whose love for us never fails. He is our Good Shepherd. He is not as the hireling who watches the sheep with no love in his heart for them, but merely for the wages that are paid. For such a shepherd is not a true shepherd. When the wolves come, he will abandon his flock and flee for his own safety. Or he will abuse the flock for his own selfish gain.

Jesus is the Good Shepherd who knows and loves his sheep. And He is known of his sheep. When He calls, they answer and they follow Him. He loves His sheep better than He loves His own life, for He is the Good Shepherd who gives His life for His sheep. Why will men and women move heaven and earth to stay out of His fold?

## 74. Lives That Lean

One of the seven wonders of the modern world is the Leaning Tower of Pisa.

Started in the year of 1174 and completed in 1350, the famous bell tower has actually been in the process of falling for many centuries.

The trouble is a slightly shifting foundation. The tower began to lean after its first three stories had been built and has kept on leaning until it is now 16½ feet out of line. It has tipped a foot in the last hundred years alone.

Efforts to arrest the "fall" by re-enforcing the base with concrete have been of no avail. Unless engineers can find a remedy not yet known, the tower is destined to fall because of its faulty foundation.

Many a life is leaning and threatened with certain fall because of a shifting foundation.

It is a well known fact, for example, that many Americans are eating themselves to death. Taking too much food into the body can be as fatal as starvation, for surplus poundage places an unnecessary burden upon the heart and the blood vessels. A diet expert tells us that the eating of one piece of bread a day beyond one's actual need can result in several pounds of surplus weight by the end of a year.

Likewise, the use of tobacco and of alcoholic beverages are known to take their toll of health and life.

Fuzzy thinking, or refusal to think and to be guided by

truth and righteousness will undermine the lives of private citizens in a democracy and, if wide spread enough, can undermine and destroy the democracy itself.

Hate, envy, jealousy, and self-centeredness, though hidden far inside one, certainly throw a life out of line and, unless remedied, result in certain fall.

In our characters, we are what we are today because of what we were yesterday, the day before yesterday, and daily across our lives. We will be tomorrow and next year and ten years from now — throughout eternity — according to what we are today.

The writer of Psalm 73 puzzled over the fact that many of the wicked apparently prosper while the righteous often seem not to fare so well. But when he went "into the sanctuary of God" he was made to see that the lives of the wicked, though they seem to thrive, are "set in slippery places" and that God will cast "them down into destruction" but "Truly God is good to Israel even to such as are of a clean heart."

The one who builds his life on Christ and His righteousness will never fall.

## 75. He Took Our Place

Once when I had misplaced the key to the corn crib and it had taken our family an hour or so to find it, Papa solemnly decreed: "Son, the next time you misplace the key I'll give you a whipping."

Just a day or two later, the key was missing again. After a brief and perfunctory search failed to turn it up, Papa turned me up. And that was back in the days of the straight-edge razor with its leather strap that could be used for purposes other than sharpening razors.

Sometime later that fateful day the key was found, hanging on a nail a boy of my stature could not even reach. The hired hand had been the culprit that time and I had taken a licking for his "crime."

Papa apologized, but the back side of my lap continued to smart for some time.

As I have thought of the whipping I received for what someone else had done, I have been reminded of Christ and the sacrifice he made for me and for you and for every other person who has lived or will live before the end of time:

"Surely he hath borne our griefs, and carried our sorrows: yet we did esteem him stricken, smitten of God, and afflicted.

"But he was wounded for our transgressions, he was bruised for our iniquities: the chastisement of our peace was upon him; and with his stripes we are healed.

"All we like sheep have gone astray; we have turned every one to his own way; and the Lord hath laid on him the iniquity of us all" (Isa. 53:4-6).

I am reminded again of the words of the penitent thief as he and his fellow robber were dying with Jesus on the crosses:

"Dost not thou fear God . . .?" he asked the other robber when that one had railed on Jesus, saying "If thou be Christ, save thyself and us."

Remarking that he and his fellow robber were on their crosses justly, the penitent thief continued: ". . . for we receive the due reward of our deeds: but this man hath done nothing amiss."

Blessed thought, wonderful assurance, ". . . he died for all, that they which live should not henceforth live unto themselves, but unto him which died for them, and rose again" (II Cor. 5:15).

75 STORIES AND ILLUSTRATIONS
FROM EVERYDAY LIFE